Westminster Directory of Public Worship

Puritans - Ministers of the World

Sinclair B. Ferguson

&

Preaching Like the Puritans:

Mark Dever

Puritans - Ministers of the World Copyright © Sinclair B. Ferguson 2008
Preaching Like the Puritans Copyright © Mark Dever 2008

ISBN 978-1-84550-427-4

10 9 8 7 6 5 4 3 2 1

Published in 2008
in the
Christian Heritage Imprint
by
Christian Focus Publications Ltd.,
Geanies House, Fearn, Ross-shire,
IV20 1TW, Scotland, Great Britain

www.christianfocus.com

Cover design by moose77.com
Printed by Norhaven A/S, Denmark

Contents

Puritans:
Ministers of the World
Sinclair B. Ferguson

Few, if any, epochs in the history of the Christian church can boast so many outstanding examples of pastoral ministry as the Puritan period of the late sixteenth and seventeenth centuries. Even a little knowledge of the history of the cure of souls underscores the impressiveness of the example of men like William Perkins, Richard Sibbes, John Bunyan, Richard Baxter, Thomas Goodwin, John Owen, Thomas Watson – and many others who, though less well known now, were revered in their own day for the power and fruitfulness of their ministries.

To turn to the work of the Puritans today, against the background of contemporary popular Christian literature, is to enter a markedly different order of reality. For those unacquainted with their writings, a first encounter with Puritan literature can be like entering a world where people seem bigger, wiser, and years older.

To read and study the Puritans is akin to standing in a familiar house and noticing there is an extra door one had never noticed. Press it open and a large basement full of unimagined resources comes into view. Here one may linger often, and from here Christians – and not least Christian pastors – may return to the world of their daily service with renewed vigor, with a greater sense of the gospel and its power, deeply challenged to live for their chief end: 'to glorify God and enjoy him for ever.'[1]

Here we find ourselves in a world of men with a clear vision of the nature of true pastoral ministry, and an unreserved commitment to it, whatever the personal cost. This is an environment of clear-sightedness, single-mindedness, and a deep love of God which, if applied to the work of the pastor today would have a profound, if at times a disturbing, impact on our understanding of the real task of the ministry.

The Puritan View of the Ministry

What lay at the heart of this Puritan view of the ministry? It was the vision of seeing godly, learned, preachers and spiritual shepherds replacing the spiritually impoverished pastoral ministries which had come to characterize much of the church in late sixteenth-century England. So successful were they in this that within half a century the quality of English clergy in general had became a byword.

Puritan ministers were, of course, varied in personality, gift, burden and sphere of calling. Indeed while they shared the same heartbeat, and while the family likeness in their ministries is obvious, there was great diversity of style among them. The insight in Phillips Brooks' notion that preaching is "the bringing of truth through personality"[2] can be abundantly illustrated in Puritan preachers. The dramatic features of a John Rogers of Dedham who

---

1. The answer to the first question in *The Shorter Catechism* produced by the Westminster Assembly.
2. Phillips Brooks, *Lectures on Preaching*, New York, 1878, p. 5.

at times would virtually "act out" his preaching in a dramatic way involved a different use of the imagination from the preaching of, for example, the story telling John Flavel, or the deep reasoning of a John Owen. But the Puritans shared a common perspective on what pastoral ministry ought to be. It was the work of men who were, first, godly and learned; second, men whose task was preaching, and who, third, in the deepest sense cared for their people.

But we can find more colorful descriptions in their own writings. No better exists than the famous word-portrait of the Puritan minister which John Bunyan gives us in Part One of his *Pilgrim's Progress.*

Christian comes to Interpreter's House where he sees a picture:

> Christian saw a picture of a very grave person hang up against the wall, and this was the fashion of it: it had eyes lift up to Heaven, the best of books in its hand, the law of truth was written upon its lips, the world was behind its back; it stood as if it pleaded with men, and a crown of gold did hang over its head.

Interpreter provided the artistic exegesis and commentary:

> The man whose picture this is, is one of a thousand; he can beget children, travail in birth with children, and nurse them himself when they are born. And whereas thou seest him with his eyes lift up to heaven, the best of books in his hand, and the law of truth writ on his lips, it is to show thee that his work is to know, and unfold dark things to sinners even as

> also thou seest him stand as if he pleaded with men; and whereas thou seest the world as cast behind him, and that a crown hangs over his head, that is to show thee that slighting and despising the things that are present, for the love that he hath to his Master's service, he is sure in the world that comes next to have glory for his reward ... this is the only man whom the Lord of the Place whither thou art going hath authorized to be thy guide in all difficult places thou mayest meet with in the way.[3]

All the ingredients of the Puritan view of the ministry can be seen in this single portrait: the basic qualification of personal godliness and giftedness coupled with single-minded learning in the interpretation of Scripture; a spirit of prayerfulness; a deep care for the people of God; and the ability to unfold the mysteries of the gospel in a manner which reached into men's hearts and touched their consciences – and all set within the context of a prayerful dependence on the Lord.

This style of ministry is never without cost. That was certainly true of the Puritans. Their lot was far from ideal. The sixteenth and seventeenth centuries were no times to be committed to biblical ministry if earthly comforts featured high on one's list of priorities – or, perhaps as importantly, on one's wife's list. Many of them suffered materially for their faithfulness to the gospel. True, some Puritans – such as John Owen – seem to have been comfortably endowed, on occasion through marriage. But these were the exception, not the rule.

Secular historians suggest that less than ten per cent of

---

3. John Bunyan, *The Pilgrim's Progress*, edited by Roger Sharrock, Harmondsworth, 1965, pp. 60-61.

churches provided a salary remotely commensurate with the Puritan minister's educational qualifications. Add to this the struggles which would, in 1662, lead to the ejection of some 2000 ministers of Puritan conviction from their livings and it becomes clear that however competent these men were, intellectually and spiritually, they did not look to, or live for, this present world. Middle-class comfort was by no means their aspiration in life.

What, then, did mark these men and their ministries?

The Puritan Minister

The marriage of true learning and personal godliness lay at the heart of the Puritan vision. A recurring note in their thinking was the apostolic injunction, 'pay careful attention to yourselves' (Acts 20:28); 'guard your life ...' (1 Tim. 4:16). Personal godliness was the great essential. The chief misery of the church, argued Richard Baxter, lies in the fact that there are too many men who are ministers before they are Christians.

And so the Puritan pastor was marked, first and foremost, by his personal growth in grace: his reading, study, knowledge of and obedience to God's Word in his own life.

But, unlike many of their predecessors and a growing number of their contemporaries, especially the so-called 'mechanik preachers,' the Puritans sought to marry *learning* to their spirituality.

In those days, theological college was as yet no part of ministerial training. Perkins, Preston, Manton, Sibbes, Cotton, Goodwin, Owen – none of these men had what we would regard as a theological education. But they were university-educated men benefiting from a system which had incorporated the study of Latin, Greek and Hebrew into the curriculum at Oxford and Cambridge Universities early in the fifteenth century. They had further equipped themselves by personal study done while serving as tutors and chaplains in wealthy homes. Often they apprenticed themselves to well-tried gospel ministers, at times lived with them, and breathed in the atmosphere of ministry by observation and personal discussion in a way that echoed the schools of the prophets in the days of Elijah and Elisha, and imitated the pattern of Paul and Timothy.

This practical training was extended on occasions when ministers would gather – often on market day – for times of public preaching and thereafter to 'combine', that is to share a fellowship meal in which younger men could eavesdrop on the rich and experienced conversation of older ministers.

In many ways these gatherings, known as 'prophesy-ings' were rooted in the practice of the weekly *congrega-tions* which John Calvin had developed in Geneva, when the local ministers and others met for weekly Bible study, often concluding with Calvin himself leading them into the meaning, significance, and application of the passage set for study. As for Calvin, so for the Puritans, "prophesy-ing" was, in essence, an exposition and application of God's word in the power of the Spirit. Thus for all practical pur-poses these regular gatherings became seminars in faith and preaching skills for younger men.

It would be mistaken, however, to think that in lacking a seminary, theological college, or divinity faculty educa-tion these men lacked a biblical and theological education itself. Their learning in areas of biblical study and theology would have left most of them unembarrassed in the company of a modern graduate in theology. Indeed, a seminary graduate sharing the ordination exam of the young ministerial candidate (later a Westminster Divine) John Carter might be taken aback by his answer to the question: 'Have you read through the Bible?' 'Yes' Carter replied, 'I have read the Old Testament twice through in the Hebrew, and the New Testament often through in the Greek.' That may have been somewhat exceptional, but Carter was by no means unique.

Of course these men lacked the benefit of the three hundred years of biblical interpretation which have passed since their time, and it would be a mistake to discount those advances. But the style of their training well illustrates the principle that it is often what takes place *outside* of the classroom that really determines the quality of preparation for ministry. Their intense familiarity with and love for Scripture provided them with an understanding of the grace of God and of the human heart which we might well envy.

That is well illustrated today by the widespread reading of such a work as John Owen's searching little book, *On the Mortification of Sin*.[4] Today regarded as strong meat for mature Christians with substantial appetites, Owen actually preached the material to students at Oxford University, many of them presumably in their late teens.

The Puritans were also well capable of highly technical biblical studies. John Owen, for example, published a commentary on Hebrews of extraordinary sophistication. But this work, which is perhaps the zenith of Puritan biblical exegesis, also abounds in practical applications. It therefore underscores the fact that the great interest lay – to coin a term

---

4. *Works of John Owen*, ed. W. H. Goold, Edinburgh, 1850-53, vol I, p. 1-86. The work was first published in 1656.

on the basis of Paul's language in 2 Timothy 3:16 – in the *ophelimostic* qualities of Scripture.[5] Their burden was not the explanation of the syntax of the texts on which they preached, but the fact that Scripture is *useful* in its power to transform character and life. Thus study of it was not for purely professional reasons such as the writing of the academic literature of which they were eminently capable, or even the writing of sermons. Rather they studied to know God. For them theology was the art of living well, and it was out of the rich fulness of the biblical knowledge they developed that they were able to speak so powerfully.

The Puritan preachers possessed a diversity of gifts – academic as well as pastoral, controversial as well as conscience-striking and comforting. But the centre of their task was offering Christ and wooing men and women to him. To this they devoted the very best of their energies and imaginative powers. Preaching, as one of them said, is the chariot that carries Christ to the world.

This Christocentric element in their thinking has often been neglected in the study of the Puritans. One only needs to think of Richard Sibbes' wonderful portrayal of a Christ who does not break the bruised reed;[6] or of Thomas Goodwin's mighty descriptions of the unveiled heart of Christ as Mediator;[7] or of John Owen's awe-inspiring and loving exposition of the glories of Jesus Christ,[8] to realise that these were Christ-full preachers.

---

5. Paul speaks about the God-breathed Scripture being 'profitable' or 'useful' (*ophelimos*). for the very practical functions of teaching, reproof, correction and training in righteousness.

6. *The Complete Works of Richard Sibbes*, ed A.B. Grosart, Edinburgh, 1862-64, vol. I, pp. 42-101. The work was first published in 1630.

7. *The Works of Thomas Goodwin*, vol. IV., Edinburgh, 1862, pp. 93-150. The work was first published in 1651.

8. Owen, *Works*, vol. 1, 1-461. The expositions were first published posthumously in 1684 and 1691

Much modern preaching and popular evangelical teaching has a tendency to give its best energies and strongest imaginative powers to exploring man, his world, and his self improvement – witness the themes of much evangelical literature and seminars. Little more than lip-service is given to the apostolic principle to preach Christ, the whole Christ and nothing but Christ and Him crucified. The 'wondrous cross' is all too little surveyed today. But that was not so with the Puritans.

The Puritan minister's chief task, then, was the preaching of the Word of God of which he was an appointed interpreter. But he was first and foremost a *pastor*; his first task was to feed and defend his sheep; the means by which he did this was by preaching. The Puritan preacher's focus therefore never lay in the personal satisfaction he gained from study, preparation and delivery. Rather it lay in the provision of spiritual food for his flock.

For that reason, Puritan manuals on the ministry focused on how to handle the Word of God both privately and publicly in such a way that hearers would be spiritually helped and nourished. While their preaching was informative and in general educative, its central function was not the communication of information but the effecting of transformation. They therefore developed their own form of rhetoric.

The Puritan Plain Style

Puritan preaching is often described as exemplifying the so-called 'plain style' – one unadorned by developed rhetorical skills. In general terms this is true, albeit preachers' styles varied from the rugged and bare to the naturally eloquent and aesthetically pleasing. But common to all forms of this style was the adoption of Paul's principle: 'we have renounced disgraceful, underhanded ways. We refuse to practice cunning or to tamper with God's word, but by the open statement of the truth we commend ourselves to everyone's conscience in the sight of God' (2 Cor. 4:2). This *phanerosis*, the setting on display of the truth, was their goal. The wisdom of this world, the enticing aesthetics of the schools of oratory and acting, were thus eschewed. No rhetorical interest or effect should stand between the hearer and the truth of the gospel.

Consequently three features were characteristic of the Puritan sermon from the time of William Perkins through the middle of the seventeenth century:

(i)   First the text was 'opened'. The preacher would brief-ly explain its meaning in its context in Scripture.
(ii) Secondly, it was 'divided'. As a diamond merchant might cut precious stones, so the preacher would separate out from the text the specific doctrines he would teach, and then verbally hold them up before the eyes of the congregation.
(iii) Thirdly, 'uses' were expounded. Great practical questions were asked and answered: 'How does this apply to me?' 'How do I know these things are true of me?' 'How can I make this mine?'

Puritan preaching therefore required three fundamental skills of the preacher himself: exegetical insight, a solid grasp of systematic theology (the 'body of divinity'), and spiritual wisdom (in order for his exegetical and theo-logical work to be applicable to the body of Christ in the world). The Puritans believed themselves to be called to be exegetes, but their preaching was not merely a re-telling of the text. They were theologians, but their aim was not the display of philosophical erudition, for they believed that all Scripture and therefore all theology belonged to all the people of God. They were also spiritual counselors, but they believed that the best counselor is the Holy Spirit who applies the word of God to our minds, consciences, emotions, dispositions and affections especially through preaching. They saw themselves as spiritual surgeons whose calling was to use the cleanest, sharpest, most appropriate instruments available to them to enable them to do a profound work through spiritual incisions that might lead to healing.

This aspect of their thinking is of great significance. The Puritan movement did not set preaching and counseling over against one another as alternatives. For them preaching *was* counseling, and the most fundamental and best counseling was done in preaching. Such preaching also, inevitably brought to the surface specific needs which might need further counsel, and so many of them spent long hours engaged in personal counseling. A further common feature of Puritan churches was a more general public counseling meetings in which ministers and mature leaders might deal with 'cases of conscience', expounding biblical teaching on Christian patterns of behavior and especially encouraging and strengthening the weak.

The Puritans would have found passing strange any 'Christian' preaching that did not bring counsel that was both biblically rooted and practically applicable. They would equally have found strange any 'Christian' counseling that did not place a fundamental emphasis on constantly sitting under a biblical ministry. Healing neuroses was not their goal; a transformed life for the glory of God was.

The Puritan pastors believed that through applicatory preaching the Holy Spirit works, without further limited human mediation, to apply the word of God to individual situations. The effectiveness of their work is evidenced by the accusations made against some of them by members of their congregations that they had hired paid informers to tell them the secrets of their hearers!

Much could be said about this. But it is worth noting that the Puritans also never divorced counseling from the life of the fellowship of the church. It was, in their view, of the essence of a congregation's life that it would be not only an army in the battles of the Lord, but also a hospital for the war-wounded.

Preaching Grids

The Puritans applied their exposition to many different needs Here they took a lead from Jesus' parable of the Sower and the Soils. The Puritan pastor knew that those who listened to him belonged to different categories of condition and need. Here, as in other respects, they took their lead from the 'preaching grid' which they found first in Jesus: the pathway, the rocky soil, the weed-infested soil, the good soil.

A more sophisticated 'grid' was found in a developed contemporary form in the great William Perkins' work *The Arte of Prophecying*.

The Arte of Prophecying had been published in 1592 in Latin – an indication that it was intended for an educated audience. It was translated into English by Thomas Tuke and published in 1606 some four years or so after Perkins' death. The influence of this little book[9] flowed

---

9. For a modernised version see *The Art of Prophesying*, including Perkins' powerful two-part tract on *The Calling of the Ministry*, ed. Sinclair B. Ferguson, Edinburgh, 1996.

partly from its own seminal character, but largely from the well-deserved reputation of its author as a preacher of unparalleled power and fruitfulness.

Such was the impact of Perkins' preaching and indeed of his very presence in the university city of Cambridge that when the young John Cotton heard the church bell tolling at Perkins' death he rejoiced that his conscience would never again be smitten by Perkins' sermons. Little did he know!

Ten years later, when the twelve-year-old Thomas Goodwin came up to Cambridge (in 1613) 'the town was then filled with the discourse of the power of Mr Perkins' ministry.'[10]

Perkins divided hearers into seven categories.

1. Ignorant and unteachable unbelievers.
2. Ignorant but teachable.
3. Knowledgeable but unhumbled.
4. The humbled, either partly or thoroughly.
5. Those who are already believers.
6. Backsliders of various kinds.
7. Congregations containing a mixture of believers and unbelievers.

What is significant here is not so much the precise details of Perkins' preaching grid – we might want to use different ones today. Rather it is his consciousness of, and sensitivity to, the differing spiritual conditions of those to whom he ministered the Word of God. He was far from having a needs-orientation in his preaching (he was more interested in *creating* a sense of need through deep conviction of

---

10. Robert Halley, 'Memoir of Thomas Goodwin, D.D.' in Goodwin's *Works*, vol. 2, Edinburgh, 1861, p xiii.

sin than in pandering to what his hearers superficially might think of as their 'needs'). Yet he clearly shaped his application of Scripture to the *specific* conditions, and to *all of the* conditions, of his hearers.

Richard Sibbes wrote in similar vein of the preacher's responsibility: 'Ministers…are *to learn their duty hence, to observe the dispositions of people, and what bars they lay to their own salvation*'[11] in order that through the ministry of the word they might deal with them faithfully.

Puritan ministers thus realised that this aspect of preaching – bringing it home to the hearers – was, as they expressed it, the most 'painful' (i.e. painstaking) aspect of both preparation and delivery. It demanded the greatest knowledge of the human heart and its foibles. Furthermore, it laid greatest demand on their imagination since it indicated the extent to which they had placed themselves under the Word.

The 'ripping up the conscience' of which Perkins and others were such masters was a hallmark of the Puritans' mastery of pastoral skills. But they did not simply berate or beat their sheep into greater self-effort. Rather, they led them on, showed them the way, held them as they took their first steps, encouraged them with gospel grace, wooing them always to Christ. They knew that emotionally powerful sermons can be preached by those who grasp what the law demands. But life-transforming sermons can be preached only by those who also have a firm grasp on how the wonder of grace operates.

The best brief summary of such 'plain style' preaching as a central aspect of the pastoral calling is, undoubtedly, found in *The Directory for Publick Worship of God* composed by the great Assembly of Divines that met at Westminster Abbey in the 1640s and over a period of four years or so produced the documents that have been foundational ever since to Presbyterian churches. These were *The Confession of Faith, The Larger Catechism, The Shorter Catechism, The Directory for Church Government* and *The Directory for Public Worship.* Since the following chapter is devoted to an extended discussion of the view of preaching outlined in *The Directory for Public Worship* it may be helpful here to set that exposition in the context of the Westminster Assembly as a whole.

The Westminster Assembly

On 12th June, 1643, the English Parliament 'thought fit and necessary to call an Assembly of learned, godly, and judicious Divines [i.e. ministers, although laymen were also present].' It had three specific aims in view:

(i) To reform the worship, discipline and government of the Church of England;

(ii) To promote church unity among the churches in England, Scotland, and the Continent;

(iii) To clarify the doctrine and revise *The Thirty-Nine Articles* of the Church of England.[12]

What lay behind this remarkable vision, and why was it felt to be so necessary in the first place?

The historical origins of the Westminster Assembly lie, in very simple terms, in the difference between the English and Scottish Reformations. The Reformation in England was not only the fruit of a widespread movement of spiritual awakening and revival in the early sixteenth century;

---

11. *Works* vol.VII, p.481.

12. See the 'Ordinance . . . for the calling of an Assembly of learned and godly Divines, and others . . ." printed in *The Confession of Faith*, 1970, p.11.

it was also intertwined with the personal life of the monarch Henry VIII, and particularly his marital status. At one time created *Defensor Fidei* by the Pope (a title the British monarch still carries), Henry would eventually resist the authority of Rome rather than bow to its judgments on his marital infidelity. The Reformation in England, subsequently, took the form of a balancing act between the new wine of the reformation gospel, and the old wine bottles of the unreformed church.[13]

Undoubtedly a further difference in the two reformations involved the personalities of the leaders of the churches in England and Scotland. There is no impersonal theology! Simply put, Scotland had John Knox.

John Knox 'The Chief Priest and Founder'

John Knox was born in Haddington probably around 1514. He studied in St Andrews and, in 1536, became a priest. Some time in the 1540s he seems to have come under the influence of Thomas Guilliame and was converted to the reformed faith. He thereafter became a friend, and sometime bodyguard, of his contemporary George Wishart. Wishart was arrested and executed in St Andrews in 1546. In a bloody story, vividly related by Knox in his *History of the Reformation in Scotland*, Wishart's death was avenged and a group of reformers gathered in St Andrews Castle whither Knox and some of his pupils came in 1547.

Despite apparent differences in temperament, Knox shared with John Calvin a desire to pursue learning, teach others, and be a faithful encourager of other leaders. But

---

13. For a detailed, scholarly account in the context of a major biography of one of the central players in the drama, see D. MacCulloch, *Thomas Cranmer: A Life,* London, 1966.

in the Castle congregation his gifts were soon recognized, and he was called to the ministry. Despite a literal flight in tears he soon became the leader of the embryonic new Scottish church.

Besieged by French gunboats called into service by Mary of Guise, Queen Regent during the early years of Mary Stuart, Queen of Scots, the Castle congregation was forced into surrender and Knox became a slave on French galleys for some eighteen months. By now he was developing into a feisty and single-minded leader.

Freed in 1549, Knox returned home to minister in Berwick, and in 1551 in Newcastle. On the death of King Edward in 1554 and the accession of 'Bloody' Mary Tudor, he fled to the Continent where he spent time ministering and studying with Calvin in Geneva (which he believed to be 'the most perfect school of Christ since the days of the apostles.').

He also ministered in Frankfort-on-Main, and there, in the context of controversy, sought to reform the church from having an 'English face' to be a church that was fully reformed according to Scripture. For Knox this meant that only what was mandated by Scripture could be mandated in congregational worship. In 1555 he spent time in Scotland where he was being increasingly looked to as the church's most experienced, and perhaps best connected, leader. He returned briefly to Geneva in 1556 (meanwhile being burnt in effigy at Edinburgh Cross). Urged in 1557 to return, he came back finally to his homeland in 1558.

A man of radical biblical conviction, extraordinary drive, and deep passion, for the next fourteen years John Knox led the very remarkable reformation that has left its imprint on the Scottish nation ever since. Absolutely convinced that the Scriptures are 'the mouth of God' he sought to apply their authority to every aspect of the church's life, not least to worship to which he applied what has come to be known as the puritan regulative principle, namely that only what God commands can carry authority in the organization, structure, and worship of the church. Knox's own explanation of the success of his labors was simply that '*God gave his Holy Spirit to simple men in great abundance.*'

As we have noted, Knox had for a period ministered in England. His opposition to aspects of the 1552 Prayer Book led to the last-minute inclusion of the so-called 'Black Rubric' affirming that kneeling at communion carried no Roman significance. In some respects this was more of a rebuttal of Knox than a victory for him. He opposed kneeling during communion either with or without explanation. Having been appointed to the team of royal chaplain preachers in 1551, in one sermon before the King he had used the occasion 'freely to attack kneeling at the Lord's Supper.' To that extent 'The Black Rubric' (so-called because it had been printed at the last minute in black rather than the customary red) it underscored the difference between the vision of an Archbishop and that of plain "Mr" Knox. That notwithstanding, Knox at one point was offered the bishopric of Rochester.

Knox and his friends were never able to establish his regulative principle in the life of the Church of England. Failure, however, did not bring about the demise of desire. Convictions about the regulative principle lingered on, took root in the lives of many in England, and effected a desire for such further reformation. All this simply confirms that there is some insight in Thomas Carlyle's comment that it is actually John Knox who was the 'Chief Priest and Founder' of English Puritanism.[14]

The 'Puritans' who shared Knox's vision (a 'purifying' of the national church) were stubbornly resisted by Elizabeth I from 1558 onwards. They were to be further disappointed when, following the Union of the Crowns in 1603, James VI of Scotland (and now James I of England) – despite his rigorous education at the hands of Scottish Calvinists – resisted the Puritan movement vehemently. His position was famously summarized in his opening statement at The Hampton Court Conference of 1611:

> If you aim at Scottish Presbytery, it agreeth as well with monarchy as God and the Devil. Then Jack and Tom and Will and Dick shall meet and censure me and my Council...My Lords the Bishops, if once you were out and they in, I know what would become of my supremacy, for No Bishop, No King. I will make them conform themselves, or I will harry them out of the land, or else do worse.

James at least knew the stomach of the people; his son, Charles I, reared by his father in the Divine Right of Kings doctrine, was altogether less sensitive. His national and foreign policies, coupled with his Roman Catholic wife and his personal life style led to increasing tensions in the nation which, coupled with the spread of the Puritan movement and its influence in Parliament, led eventually to the Civil War.

---

14. *Heroes and Hero Worship in The Works of Thomas Carlyle*, vol.5, London, 1907, p. 143.

The Assembly

It was in the context of such political and social tension, indeed virtually as part of it, that the idea of a reforming assembly was first mooted. Charles eventually forbade it, but the Assembly at Westminster nevertheless convened – albeit minus the presence of Archbishop James Ussher and others who shared his Episcopalian perspective).

Strictly speaking the Assembly was a parliamentary advisory body. A list of potential participants had been drawn up more than a year earlier (two ministers from each English county, the two English Universities, and one for each Welsh county, plus four from the city of London, with a further fourteen others named by the Lords. In addition twenty laymen from the House of Commons and ten from the House of Lords were chosen). Despite the royal proclamation on 22 June 1643 prohibiting the Assembly, Parliament proceeded with its own Ordinance. And so the Assembly held regular meetings at Westminster Abbey in London, meeting at first in Henry VII's Chapel, until, with the onset of winter, the plenary sessions were moved to the Jerusalem Chamber (which boasted a fireplace!).

Later in the year a group of Scottish ministers and elders arrived to assist in the work. Although they were never technically members of the Assembly, in many ways they were the most powerful single group participating in it and virtually became a kind of approval committee for the work that was transacted. They included several of the most famous Scottish ministers of the seventeenth century, Alexander Henderson, Samuel Rutherford, and the remarkably gifted young George Gillespie.

The progress of the Assembly, recorded in its Minutes and in other extant materials written by participants, was marked by tension among the various ecclesiastical parties (Presbyterians of various stripes, Independents who resisted the strong connectionalism of the former, and a group of Erastians who held a strong view of state authority in relationship to the church). The Scots Commissioner Robert Baillie in particular found the devotion to detailed argument a drain on his patience: 'nothing in any Assemblie that was in the world except Trent, like to this in prolixitie', he wrote home to Scotland![15]

In the first weeks of the Assembly much attention was given to the task of revising the Church of England's *Thirty-Nine Articles*. The Divines had proceeded to discuss about one third of these when *The Solemn League and Covenant* was entered into as a religious bond between Scotland and England. And it became clear that something more comprehensive than a mere revision would be necessary. Parliament now instructed the Divines to proceed immediately to the production of Directories for both Church Government and Public Worship. Having begun with the former, the latter was discussed at various times during 1644. Once completed the Directory was approved by the General Assembly of the Church of Scotland in February 1645.

It is one of the ironies of the entire Assembly that while the Scots made various compromises of their own traditions, by and large the impact of the Assembly on the English Church was minimal whereas it marked Scottish Church life for centuries to come.

The regular pattern of the Assembly was for the Divines to meet in plenary sessions in the mornings and was divided into three committees for the purpose of drafting materials which would then be debated on the floor of the

---

15. *Letters and Journals of Robert Baillie*, Edinburgh 1842, vol. 2, p. 104.

entire gathering. Debate on various points of doctrine and liturgy stretched over several days on some occasion as the Assembly sought to express biblical teaching in a manner that carried the wide agreement of the whole body. We often think of 'compromise wording' as a feature of liberal theology, but, clearly, one of the challenges facing the Divines at Westminster was to create statements of doctrine and practice that placed most emphasis on major elements of agreement and minimized differences over matters that did not so obviously belong to the heart of biblical teaching, or involved more abstract reasoning. What was true in areas of doctrinal expression was also characteristic of their approach to liturgy.

The Directory for Public Worship

The Directory for Public Worship was intended to produce a more uniform ethos in worship. It covered such matters as the behavior of the congregation, conduct of worship, prayers, forms of administration of baptism and communion, marriage, pastoral visiting of the sick, burial of the dead, fasting, thanksgiving and praise.

There were 'worship wars' in the seventeenth century as well as our own. Some of them were fought out behind the scenes of the Assembly. Frequently issues arose about the proper application of the Puritan regulative principle which reduced elements of acceptable worship to what is prescribed or necessarily deducible from Scripture alone. Disagreements over how communion should be served, patterns of devotion and other details abounded. The final document is in many ways a fine example of compromise on non-essentials set within the context of agreement on essentials.

Without doubt one of the Directory's most relevant sections is its discussion of preaching. The chairman of the committee to whom the drafting of the Directory was given was Stephen Marshall (1594?-1655) himself one of the greatest of the Puritan preachers. The Directory was finally approved by Parliament in January 1645.

The Directory's outline of what is involved in the exposition of Scripture could fruitfully be engraved onto the desk of every preacher of the gospel. Wisely their instruction was framed in a way that made it applicable to a whole range of preaching methods and styles (a range, incidentally, to which the Puritans themselves gave rich expression. Homiletical cloning, was not their purpose any more than it should be ours):

> This method is not prescribed as necessary for every man, or upon every text [he is likely to be a homiletical cripple who does not realize or has not heard evidence of the fact that some sermons of startling power seem to break most homiletical rules!]; but only recommended, as being found by experience to be very much blessed of God, and very helpful for the people's understandings and memories.

These principles were, in their view, as applicable to preaching from one text, an entire passage, a key doctrinal statement, as they were to preaching systematically through a section or entire book of Scripture.

A brief introduction should lead the preacher to a summary or paraphrase of the preaching segment and to the principal burden of the exposition. Sensitive to the mental capacity of his hearers, the preacher should feed them well but never overload them. In particular the following three rules were seen to be fundamental:

1. What is taught must be biblical truth. But more than that, it must be drawn from the text or passage being expounded, so that people can see for themselves that it is biblical and how they themselves can draw that truth from the same Scripture.

These men recognized that, as a general rule, the way Christians read the Bible privately is shaped by the model of exposition they regularly hear from the pulpit. That is why this principle is not only essential to the integrity of pastoral preaching but central to the whole ethos of a congregation's life.

2. The teaching on which the passage focuses should then be highlighted, expounded and illustrated and honest and relevant difficulties (intellectual or practical) dealt with. The preacher is not a purveyor of novelties nor is his task to titillate some in his congregation with the latest deviation in the evangelical world, nor to set on display his own erudition. He is behind the 'sacred desk' to teach and to nourish the flock. As a general principle whatever is not edifying and spiritually nourishing should be no part of the preacher's message.

3. Stage three brings the preacher in the study to his knees. He must not only make clear the burden of the passage, but also, in the words of the Westminster Divines,

> bring it home to special use, by application to his hearers ... a work of great difficulty to himself, requiring much prudence, zeal and meditation, and to the natural and corrupt man ... very unpleasant; yet he is to endeavour to perform it in such a manner,

that his auditors may feel the word of God to be quick and powerful, and a discerner of the thoughts and intents of the heart; and that, if any unbeliever or ignorant person be present, he may have the secrets of his heart made manifest, and give glory to God.

How is this to be done? The Westminster masters stressed three further things:

(i) In the light of the grace of God in the gospel, the Puritan minister spelled out the 'duties' found in Scripture. 'Duty' is a much-misunderstood term in our modern culture and carries with it the aroma of legalism. In contrast the Puritan minister realised that grace always leads to and commands duties; he was a Paulinist in this sense – all his imperatives were rooted in the indicatives of grace; but every indicative of grace gave rise in his preaching to an imperative of grace-filled obedience.

So far have contemporary Christians slipped in grasping the shape and logic of the gospel that when they discover that some fifty per cent of the *Shorter Catechism* is taken up expounding the law the cry of 'legalism' is often heard. But the Puritan pastor saw that it is in the fulfillment of the duties of grace that grace comes into its own. So he labored to make clear how these duties may be fulfilled in love and joy suffused with a glorious pleasure in walking with God in ways that honor him. After all, the Scriptures teach us how to live for God's glory and in doing so to enjoy Him.

(ii) The gospel minister further must unveil the true nature of sin with its misery, danger and remedy. Virtually every sermon will strike this note in one form or another. Anselm's words to Boso, the theological stooge in the former's famous *Cur Deus Homo*, echoed from every Puritan pulpit in the seventeenth century: 'You have not yet considered the greatness of the weight of sin.'[16]

The Puritans treated this as a pastoral as well as a theological formula: grace makes sense to us only in the light of the sin to which it provides the remedy. Consequently, the more sensitive we are to sin, misery and danger, the more clearly we will grasp the wonder of God's salvation. Grace is only 'amazing' when we see that it is 'a *wretch* like me' it saves. Only sinners seek Jesus as a Savior!

Nor did the Puritan stop there. To borrow William Gurnall's words, the Christian needed to be equipped with 'complete armour'[17]; against temptation. This the preacher furnished from Scripture, in addition to providing comfort and encouragement for the afflicted and assailed heart. He took human problems seriously, analysed them in the light of Scripture and resolved them from the same source.

(iii) Puritan preachers also gave what they called 'notes of trial'. Here the Westminster Divines' description of this aspect of preaching illumines the practical value of reflecting on the Perkinsian 'categories' mentioned earlier:

It is sometimes requisite to give some notes of trial (which is very profitable, especially when performed by able and experienced ministers, with circumspection and prudence, and the signs clearly grounded on the holy scripture,) whereby the hearers may be able to examine themselves whether they have attained those graces, and performed those duties, to which he exhorteth, or be guilty of the sin reprehended, and

---

16. Anselm, *Cur Deus Homo*, chapter xxi.
17. The expression is drawn from the title of Gurnall's famous work *The Christian in Complete Armour*, London, 1655-1662.

in danger of the judgments threatened, or are such to whom the consolations propounded do belong; that accordingly they may be quickened and excited to duty, humbled for their wants and sins, affected with their danger, and strengthened with comfort, as their condition, upon examination, shall require.

This, then, was the Puritan preaching 'method'. As we have noted, they did not regard this as an unbreakable preaching rule, or a method of cloning preachers – no one familiar with their sermons would confuse John Owen with Thomas Watson for example! So long as the Scriptures were truly expounded and applied – by whatever method – the key lay in the extent to which the preacher himself was given over to, and himself sat under, the Word. As Owen wrote, 'No man preacheth that sermon well to others that doth not first preach it to his own heart'[18]

What did this imply? These seven things:

(i) A commitment to the hard work of studying, meditating on, applying to oneself the truth of Scripture.

(ii) A concern to speak God's truth to all of God's people, however simple they might be. The great Puritans were well-educated and highly intelligent ministers; but they knew that the concealment of art is also an art.

(iii) Preaching the whole counsel of God, for the conversion of men and women, for the glory of God alone in whose presence both great and obscure must be exposed as sinners;

(iv) Manifesting wisdom in teaching and applying the Word of God, as well as the grace of God in the very spirit of the preaching without 'passion or bitterness'.

18. John Owen, *Works*, ed. W. Goold, IX. p. 155.

(v) Doing so with a sense of the *gravitas* which ought to characterise a servant of God. This influenced the minister's physical demeanor and even the use of his voice. The preacher is neither joker nor trifler. He is not sent by God to entertain and amuse, for life is more of a tragedy than a comedy. Message and manner must harmonise or the message itself will be trivialised. Emotions and affections in preaching must be consistent with and expressive of the very substance of the text which is being expounded.

(vi) Neither is the minister to be lugubrious and censorious, but rather filled with a loving affection for those to whom he ministers and preaches. Nothing is better calculated to win hearers than their knowledge that their minister has 'a hearty desire to do them good'. The Puritans recognised that people will take a great deal from such a man.

(vii) All this is backed up by a life which is consistent both in private and in public with the message that is preached.

All this, the Puritans emphasized, should ordinarily be anchored in a local context where the preacher fed a flock he had come to know and love.

Local Ministry

There were three obvious reasons that it was essential to the Puritans that a minister should be *resident* among his people, not absent from them.

(i) The calling of the Puritan minister was to feed the flock in his charge through the ministry of the Word.

(ii) In apostolic fashion that was always coupled with prayer, without which the wheels of the chariot in which Christ was conveyed to the congregation (i.e. the preaching) would not run on smooth ground.

It is impossible to overstress the importance of this principle in Puritan practice. Apostolic ministry must exemplify the apostolic principle: 'We will devote ourselves to prayer and to the ministry of the word' (Acts 6:4 ESV). For them the order was important. If the pastor was not a man of prayer he was not a true pastor. This was why Robert Traill was able to write:

> Ministers must pray much, if they would be successful...
> Some ministers of meaner gifts and parts [i.e. abilities]
> are more successful than some that are far above them
> in abilities; not because they preach better, so much as
> because they pray more. Many good sermons are lost
> for lack of much prayer in study.[19]

A further evidence of this in Puritan ministry was seen in the importance they placed on prayer in the lives of their fellowships. Richard Baxter was by no means unique in seeing it as so central that he spent one night every week gathering young people together in order that they might learn what it is to pray.

(iii) The need to particularise pastoral ministry, one aspect of which was to pray for the people, was then taken one stage further: the minister was also called to apply biblical truth to his congregation individually in personalised instruction and evangelism.

How was this accomplished? The Puritan answer was twofold. Part of it was by meeting with members of the congregation corporately outside of the context of worship. Again Baxter is an obvious example. Every Thursday

---

19. Robert Traill, *By what Means may Ministers best win Souls?* (sermon preached in October 1682 at the Cripplegate Morning Exercise), *Works,* Edinburgh, 1810, I, p.246.

night at home he gathered a group who would go over his previous sermon on the previous Lord's Day, and discuss its meaning and application.

In the recovery of biblical exposition that has marked the church in our own time, it has not always been recognized that in addition to such exposition the Reformers and Puritans placed great stress on catechising. We tend to think of this as children learning catechetical questions and answers by rote. But what the Puritans had in view was in many ways a more profound exercise. They saw the need to build into the thinking of their people frameworks of reference, grids that would help them receive, understand, digest and apply the biblical teaching given from the pulpit.

This is an essential ingredient in the recovery of biblical Christianity. Neither the Reformers nor the Puritans thought of their task as the public exposition of Scripture without finding ways of anchoring what was heard in the minds and memories of their hearers. Without the framework of doctrine provided in some such pedagogical tool as a catechism a person might find it extremely difficult to assimilate all they were being taught. And without the personal probing of catechetical questions they might never work through into practical understanding and application the public exposition.

The Baxter Plan
Richard Baxter had two catechists in Kidderminster to share in what was in part a sophisticated, well grounded kind of seventeenth-century *Evangelism Explosion*. But it was more. It was also a *Pastoral Explosion* with a fully-orbed Pauline goal: to present every man mature before God.

It was in large measure due to his vision for this work that Baxter wrote his justly famous work *The Reformed Pastor*.

His concern was to share with his ministerial brethren the necessity of pastoral visitation and personal instruction and evangelism.

The experiences which brought him to this conviction are telling. 'It hath oft grieved my heart' wrote Baxter 'to observe some eminent able preachers, how little they do for the saving of souls, save only in the pulpit; and to how little purpose much of their labour is, by this neglect.'[20]

In fact Baxter had come to the sobering personal discovery that many of his hearers were taking in far less of what he said than he imagined. He realized that he needed to speak with them one by one to help them understand the message of the gospel and to help them work out its significance for their lives. In a moment of tremendous candor, he writes:

> For my part, I study to speak as plainly and movingly as I can ... and yet I frequently meet with those that have been my hearers eight or ten years, who know not whether Christ be God or man, and wonder when I tell them the history of his birth and life and death, as if they had never heard it before. And of those who know the history of the gospel, how few are there who know the nature of that faith, repentance, and holiness which it requireth, or, at least, who know their own hearts ... I have found by experience, that some ignorant persons, who have been so long unprofitable hearers, have got more knowledge and remorse of conscience in half an hour's close discourse, than they did from ten year's public preaching.[21]

---

20. R. Baxter, *The Reformed Pastor* (1656), ed. William Brown, London, 1829, pp. 178-9.
21. Baxter, p. 196

It was this discovery that led Baxter to arrange for every family in his parish area to have a catechism and together with his two assistants he spent two days of each week, from morning until evening, moving from house to house in his parish, teaching, gently quizzing, and with great sensitivity leading people to Christ and to the Scriptures.

The effect on the town during Baxter's fifteen-year ministry was revolutionary. He states that when he was installed as rector at Kidderminster perhaps one family in each street was devoted to the Lord and honored him in family worship; when he left there were streets where only one family did not do so.

Doubtless Baxter's gifts were unusual and perhaps the blessing of God was exceptional; but it is evident that he and others felt that the instrument of catechizing was utterly essential to the work of the pastoral ministry.

Baxter knew that there would be objections to such activity. Perhaps we might be inclined to say that in Baxter's day, 'He had all the time in the world'. But not so. He tells us that when he began this work he was already fully employed (think of his well-over 100 published works, of the great folio volumes of his writings, of his magnificent *The Saints' Everlasting Rest* whose 1000 pages might seem to require experience of its title to complete a reading!).

No, Baxter saw catechizing as a work of necessity not as an additional luxury. Furthermore he recognized that beginning such an activity would cause all kinds of disturbance, but argued: anything new has that effect. Nothing ventured, nothing gained.

With Baxter, the Puritans in general realised that we cannot build for eternity with wood hay and stubble; we must build with precious stones that will last. That may be by the use of a catechism or by some similar means. By whatever means, access must be gained to the minds, hearts and homes of the people by those who are the pastors of the flock. After all the Good and Great Shepherd catechised his little flock regularly in order to test, confirm and strengthen the effect of his ministry. Something of the same order, however contemporary its garb, is surely needed today.

The Heart of the Matter

It is not surprising, then, since establishing such a preaching ministry was their goal, that so many of the Puritan ministers note the sheer costliness of this task, and echo the cry of Paul, 'Who is sufficient for these things?' They rested their souls on the apostle's answer: 'Our sufficiency is from God.'

Yet, for all the costliness of such a ministry, Puritan ministers were tremendously conscious of the privilege of the high calling they had received.

One such was Herbert Palmer (1601-47), the gifted upper-class bachelor who became one of the Assessors of the Westminster Assembly. He was widely believed to be its best catechist.

Palmer himself knew what it was to be catechized. Asked when he was only a five year old what he wanted to be he replied that he hoped to be a minister. When others tried to dissuade him by telling him that ministers were 'hated, despised, and accounted as the off scouring of the world', little Palmer nobly replied 'It was no matter for that; for if the world hated him, yet God would love him.'[22]

Perhaps more than anything else, this was the heartbeat of Puritan ministry at its best.

---

22. Samuel Clarke, *The Lives of Thirty-Two English Divines*, London, 1677, 3rd. ed., p.184.

The love of Christ constrained them to be ambassadors. That constraint invested their preaching with impassioned appeal.

The fact that their ministry was that of an ambassador drove them to the study of their Sovereign's message.

The knowledge that their Master was the Sovereign Lord gave them confidence that their mission would not, indeed could not, in the last analysis, fail.

This was the spirit that had gripped little Palmer from his earliest days.

Well might we pray today, 'Lord, will you not raise up Herbert Palmers in our day too?'

Preaching Like the Puritans

Mark Dever

The Puritans and Preaching

The Westminster Directory of Public Worship represents a flowering of Puritan understanding on topics such as the public reading of scripture, public prayer, and the preaching of the Word. The best way to introduce you to the Puritans' thinking is to urge you to read the pages that follow, in which the Puritans speak for themselves. By way of introduction, I would like to share with you the fruit of my own reflection on the text of the *Directory*, particularly those portions which address the topic of preaching.

Who were the Puritans? The word itself is notoriously difficult to define. For the purposes of this essay, the term "Puritan" simply refers to those reformed English Christians who were especially concerned with refining and purifying the church in the two hundred years or so following the Reformation.

Many people have formed negative assessments of the Puritans, perhaps relying on images from Hawthornian fiction rather than accurate historical accounts. Such negative assessments include Thomas B. Macaulay's observations in his *History of England*: "The Puritan hated bear-baiting, not because it gave pain to the bear, but because it gave pleasure to the spectators."[1] Or, as H.L. Mencken put it, "Puritanism [was] the haunting fear that someone, somewhere may be happy."[2] For a more modern negative assessment, we have the words of Garrison Keillor: "Puritans... arrived in America in 1648 in the hope of discovering greater restrictions than were permissible under English law."[3]

These false caricatures are nothing more than distortions of the Puritan tradition – amusing to many readers, perhaps, but serious in their accusations and ultimately misleading. So much more could be said about the great movement we know as the "Puritans."

I cannot begin to describe the significance of Puritanical life and thought in these few pages. Instead of offering an overview, I will focus on one aspect of the Puritans' worship – their preaching. The Puritans regarded preaching as central to the Christian mission, and they were known as great preachers. They earned excellent reputations for their handling of the Word of God. Though we no longer know most of their names, the fruits of their ministries are still with us: men such as Ezekiel Culverwell, James Nalton, Philip Nye, and literally hundreds of others.

These Puritans were not all of one mind on everything that had to do with preaching. So Nye, for instance, "held the curious view that, at sermons, the preacher should wear his hat, the audience being uncovered; at sacraments

---

1. Thomas Babington Macaulay, *The History of England from the Accession of James the Second,* Philadelphia, 1861, Vol. I, p. 47

2. *A Mencken Chrestomathy* New York, 1967, p. 624.

3. Garrison Keillor, Statement to the Senate Subcommittee on Education, 29 March 1990 (Testimony on NEA Grant Funding and Restrictions) 136 Cong. Rec. E. 993 (1990).

the minister should be bareheaded and the communicants covered."[4] Such curiosities may amuse us, but will not detain us. Instead of highlighting the variations among Puritan preachers, we will focus on the main things which the Puritans as a whole would say to us about preaching.

It will come as no surprise to the reader that the Puritans' united thoughts are quite clearly expressed in the *Westminster Directory for Public Worship.* The *Directory*, like the Confession and the Catechism which bear the Westminster name, contains a wealth of insight on topics relevant to the church in any age. Its brevity and clarity make it palatable even to the modern reader beset by busy-ness and multiple distractions. For readers of this essay, I particularly commend the few pages devoted to the preaching of the word (pp. 93-99).

The Puritans on Preaching: Describing Their Approach
The following summary of the Puritans' perspective on preaching, preachers, and sermons provides a preview of the comments you will read in the *Directory* itself. Following this preview, we will examine in greater depth the Puritans' perspective on controversy, application, and method in preaching.

Concerning preaching, the Puritans said that *preaching matters.* They believed that preaching is important enough to the preacher and to the audience that it should be done well. The value of preaching has been called into question by many in our day, yet the Puritan witness affirms the significance of preaching in the carrying out of public worship. Concerning preachers, the Puritans said that *not just anyone can preach.* The preacher is to be gifted and is to make

---

4. *Dictionary of National Biography*, New York, 1895, p. 281.

use of his gifts. This involves prayer, the study of Scriptures and of the world at large, and reliance on the Spirit.

The Puritan commentary on sermons is more extensive and addresses the selection of texts, the nature of introductions, and appropriate sermon structure. The Puritans said that sermon texts can be selected either by series or special occasions. Thus, acceptable topics for a sermon may be demanded by an expositional series or by a special occasion. Sermon introductions should be short and directly related to the text at hand. The structure of sermons, simply put, should be "text, then truths." That is, the text should first be summarized, and then doctrines can be drawn from it.

The Puritans made four main stipulations about the content of sermons. First, sermons should be faithful to the text, and should deal with sentences rather than individual words. That is, sermons should not be mere lexical exercises, but should deal with the central point of the text. Second, sermons should be true, biblical, and helpful. Sermons should make sense, flow plainly from the text, and edify the listeners. Third, sermons should be clear. Doctrine should be expressed clearly. The doctrine is not only to flow clearly from the text (see above), but also it is to be clearly *expressed*. Fourth, every part of the sermon matters. The whole sermon should be good. This includes everything from solid arguments to effective illustrations.

In addition to these basic guidelines for preaching, the Puritans offer advice about specific issues that preachers face. These issues of dealing with controversy, assisting the listeners in application, and method in preaching are timely even now, and further consideration of the Puritans' insights should prove fruitful.

The Puritans on Preaching: Controversy

The Puritans knew how to fight. They were often engaged in controversy and did not shy away from engaging contemporary issues. Nevertheless, they caution preachers to *pick their fights carefully* when addressing their congregations. What does this look like? To begin, the preacher must discern potential difficulties with the text at hand, identifying areas that his particular listeners might find troublesome. These potential difficulties can be divided into two types: those seen to be real, which must be dealt with thoroughly, and those seen to be imaginable, but either uncommon or nearly non-existent. This latter type should be ignored in the sermon itself so as not to confuse other listeners and to seek the whole congregation's edification. These are the kinds of questions that can be addressed one-on-one, perhaps at the end of the service while the preacher is greeting people at the door. It is only the first type of difficulty, which involves false doctrines that are currently dangerous, that are to be answered, and the preacher is to make every effort to answer these doctrines *well*.

Of course, the history of Puritanism and therefore of its preaching is littered with controversy, from the controversy over vestments in the middle of the sixteenth century, to the Antinomian controversy in seventeenth-century New England, with many others besides. Certainly, these preachers were not seeking out new controversies, for they understood themselves to have plenty to contend with as it was. So from the constant fears of encroaching Roman Catholicism in Old England, to Jonathan Edwards' alarms about Arminianism in New England, controversy was at home in the Puritan pulpit; but this was the case only insofar as it was deemed *needful*.

On March 30, 1642, a London preacher of some note named Simeon Ashe preached before the House of Commons at their solemn fast. Addressing these representatives of the State assembled in Parliament, he brought before them a complaint about their own employees – the bishops who were employed by the state. He said of these bishops:

> What county, what city, what town, what village, yea, what family, I had almost said, what person in the kingdom, hath not in one kind or other, in some degree or other, at one time or other, been oppressed by them? They and their officers, by citations, censures, exactions, have been Catholick oppressors. How many wealthy men have been crushed by their cruelty? How many poor families have been ruined by their tyranny? And I beseech you to consider, whether the most pious both among preachers and people, have not met with the hardest measures, from their heavy hands. Alas, alas! How many faithful ministers have they silenced? How many gracious Christians have they excommunicated! How many congregations have they starved or dissolved in this kingdom! For the proof of all this, and of more than all this, I appeal unto the many petitions presented to this honourable Parliament.[5]

These words and their accompanying tone make it clear that the Puritans as a group did not shrink from controversies which they saw as important when they were speaking in public. They did not just complain in private while conforming in public. Instead, they brought their grievances

---

5. James Reid, *Memoirs of the Westminster Divines*, (Paisley, 1811; rpt. Banner of Truth; Edinburgh, 1982) pp. 126–127.

out in public, before those who were responsible to redress them.

On this point, the Westminster Assembly's *Directory* reads as follows:

> If any doubt obvious from Scripture, reason, or preju-dice of the hearers, seem to arise, it is very requisite to remove it, by reconciling the seeming differences, answering the reasons, and discovering and taking away the causes of prejudice and mistake. Otherwise it is not fit to detain the hearers with propounding or answering vain or wicked cavils, which, as they are endless, so the propounding and answering of them doth more hinder than promote edification.
>
> ...In confutation of false doctrines, he is neither to raise an old heresy from the grave, nor to men-tion a blasphemous opinion unnecessarily: but, if the people be in danger of an error, he is to confute it soundly, and endeavor to satisfy their judgements and consciences against all objections.[6]

That is, preachers are not only encouraged to take on con-troversial issues; they are *required* to do so in the Puritan conception of the pastorate. Yet superfluous arguments are to be avoided. An example of an "old heresy from the grave" might be a contemporary rebuttal of Arianism.

When we compare the Puritan's view to the revelation in Scripture, we see that the Puritans have been faithful students of the Word on this point. The New Testament commends such work by the speaker on the behalf of expectant listen-ers. Jesus often clears difficulties from the text when he is

---

6. See p. 95–96 of this book.

addressing others. For instance, in the Sermon on the Mount (see Matt. 6), Jesus clears away Pharisaical defenses of self-righteousness. Paul clears certain objections and not others in Galatians, and we see the same techniques in the letter to the Hebrews.

I have to admit that I have not always exercised wisdom in this matter. In particular, I recall a time when the Cambridge Intercollegiate Christian Union asked me to preach a series of evangelistic sermons for students at Cambridge. I did a wretched job! Because I used to be an agnostic, I spoke to those gathered as though they too were agnostic! I imagined that they had every objection to Christianity that you could ever think of. So instead of offering them the gospel, I gave them a catalogue of objections to the gospel, along with some fairly lame responses to those objections. I certainly did not give them what many Christian students had hoped that I would present to their unbelieving friends! This is exactly what the *Directory* advises us *not* to do. Instead of letting extraneous matters determine the message, preachers should focus on the objections that are most likely to be held by those who will be listening. Preachers will certainly not bless their hearers by coming up with all kinds of arguments that the listeners may have never thought of, in order to instruct them out of problems they may never have had before they listened to the preaching! The *Directory* offers sound advice on this matter.

The Puritans on Preaching: Application

The role of application in preaching is an important theme for the Puritans, and we will highlight it here as well. The Puritans are very clear on this point, and some of their statements challenge current thinking. We will examine six statements that the Puritans make about application.

- Application is essential.
- Application should be practical.
- Application should deal with sin fully.
- Application should comfort fully.
- Application should cause self-examination.
- Application should relate to helpful doctrines drawn from the text.

Application is essential

The Puritans believed that application is an essential aspect of preaching. They remind us that doctrine must never be left unapplied. Furthermore, they urge preachers to use argument and not just sentiment in support of particular applications. Application involves more than having emotional empathy with hearers; it also involves thinking clearly about what sin is and what God is exhorting us to in His Word.

William Perkins, in his early work on preaching called *The Arte of Prophesying*, said that the preacher should remind himself of the different kinds of people that are hearing each sermon. There are those who are unbelievers and who are unteachable: they need explosions put under them! There are those who are teachable but ignorant, and so need the application particularly clearly spelled out in detail for them. There are those who have some accurate knowledge but who are not yet humbled. For them the truth preached must be applied in a way which rips up their conscience. And there are those who are humbled already: for these the preacher must bring comfort and encouraging applications. They must be shown that the Lord accepts weak faith. Then, there are believers who need to understand the gospel as it touches justification and sanctification and perseverance. They need to be taught to be holy. And there are those who are fallen, whether in their faith, or in their lives, perhaps into heresy, through a mistake, or sin through disobedience. It is the obligation of the preacher to work out applications of the truth which encourage their recovery. Finally, there are those other people mingled in, those whom the preacher may not know well, whose hearts therefore are hidden, and to them the truth of the gospel needs to be spelled out clearly. All of these groups, Perkins argued, should have application laid out particularly for them.

In the *Directory*, written forty years later, we read the following admonition:

> [The preacher] is not to rest in general doctrine, although never so much cleared and confirmed, but to bring it home to special use, by application to his hearers: which albeit it prove a work of great difficulty to himself, requiring much prudence, zeal and meditation, and to the natural and corrupt man will be very unpleasant; yet he is to endeavour to perform it in such a manner, that his auditors may feel the word of God to be quick and powerful, and a discerner of the thoughts and intents of the heart; and that, if any unbeliever or ignorant person be present, he may have the secrets of his heart made manifest, and give glory to God.
>
> In the use of instruction or information in the knowledge of some truth, which is a consequence from his doctrine, he may (when convenient) confirm it by a few firm arguments from the text in hand, and other places of scripture, or from the na-

ture of that commonplace in divinity, whereof that truth is a branch.[7]

The Westminster Directory imitates the model of Scripture in this area. In his letter to the Colossians, Paul lays out wonderful doctrine, and then applies it very specifically to their situation. He does the same in Ephesians. In I Corinthians 13, we read about the applications that spring from a heart of love. In I Peter, we see Peter applying great truths to different categories of hearers, such as people in very difficult circumstances. And James, in James 1-2, shows us how dangerous unapplied truth is. He illustrates this Puritan principle, namely, that application is essential.

Today, preachers face the twin dangers of Hypocritical Christianity and Hypothetical Theology, which both result in lives unaffected by truths unapplied. Preachers sometimes think it more spiritual only to declare objective realities of the historical work of God through Christ, and not to address the Spirit's work of application in the hearts of hearers. Some decry such applicatory work as subjectivism, pietism, or the seed bed of legalism and works-righteousness. While such perversions may, in fact, arise, they are nevertheless perversions, and not the simple application itself, the application we see in Scripture. When we oppose application as such, we are certainly separating ourselves from the understanding of the Bible and its truths that the Westminster divines had.

Application should be practical
The Puritans maintained that sermon application is only effective if the listeners can actually apply it in their own

---

7. See p. 95 of this book.

lives. Thus, applications must be practical. This involves not only telling people *what* they should do in response to a particular doctrine, but also helping them see *how* they might do it.

For example, William Gouge's eldest son, Thomas, was a minister like his father; Thomas published some of the fruit of his pulpit work on Matthew 10:41-42. In this passage, Christ encourages believers to receive a prophet or give a cup of cold water in His name. The younger Gouge goes on to develop carefully what this means in terms of almsgiving, a practice common among his listeners.

Another preacher who was always very practical in his sermons was that supreme Puritan doctor of the soul, the incomparable Richard Sibbes. On the ever-vexed pastoral question of assurance, Sibbes taught that in order to grow, one should "attend upon the ordinances of God, and use all kinds of spiritual means."[8] This included attending the preaching of the Word, meditating on it, reading the Bible and other good books, keeping good company, and taking care not to grieve the Holy Spirit.[9] The conscience must be heeded,[10] and the Word heard, must be obeyed.[11] To those attempting to regain assurance *after* sin – which he called "wilful breeches in sanctification" – Sibbes taught that "Such must give a sharp sentence against themselves, and yet cast themselves upon God's mercy in Christ, as at their first conversion."[12]

---

8. *The Complete Works of Richard Sibbes* ed. A. B. Grosart, Edinburgh, 1862-64, vol III, p. 480.

9. Ibid. pp. 480-481; cf. Geoffrey F. Nuttall, *The Holy Spirit in Puritan Faith and Experience,* (Oxford, 1946), 23-24.

10. Richard Sibbes, The Demand of a Good Conscience, *Works* (vol. 7), p. 486.

11. Richard Sibbes, Witness of Salvation, *Works* (vol. 7), p. 383; cf. Sibbes, Excellency of the Gospel Above the Law, *Works* (vol. 4), pp. 296-297; Faith Triumphant, *Works* (vol. 7), pp. 432, 436-437; Bowels Opened, *Works* (vol. 2), p. 26; Angels' Acclamation, *Works* (vol. 6), p. 354.

In situations where one was not sure of the reason for a lack of assurance, Sibbes taught that one first looked for those extraordinary and obvious signs, joy in the Holy Ghost and peace of conscience.[13] Yet, the Christian knew that when he "finds not extraordinary comfort from God's Spirit, that God's love is constant," he could reason from God's past love to God's present love.[14] The believer should be encouraged by the work of sanctification in life, however small. "Be not discouraged, when the stamp in wax is almost out, it is current in law. Put the case the stamp of the prince be an old coin (as sometimes we see it on a king Harry groat), yet it is current money, yea, though it be a little cracked."[15] Still other times, Sibbes says, friends "can read our evidences better than ourselves."[16] All of this advice is quite practical.

Nevertheless, Sibbes was intent on not minimizing the gracious nature of Christian salvation. At such times when comfort was wanting, Sibbes said, "We must judge ourselves ... by faith, and not by feeling; looking to the promises and word of God, and not to our present sense and apprehension."[17] Like Calvin, Sibbes, too, had taught that even the best actions of the believer "need Christ to perfume them...."[18] Relying too much on works was always

12. Richard Sibbes, Bruised Reed, *Works* (vol. 1), p. 70; cf. Soul's Conflict with Itself, *Works* (vol. 1), pp. 123-124, 234.

13. Richard Sibbes, Learned Commentary ... upon the First Chapter of the Second Epistle . . . to the Corinthians, *Works* (vol. 3), p. 459; cf. A Glimpse of Glory, *Works* (vol. 7), p. 96.

14. Richard Sibbes, Learned Commentary . . . upon the First Chapter of the Second Epistle ... to the Corinthians, *Works* (vol. 3), p. 459.

15. Richard Sibbes, Learned Commentary ... upon the First Chapter of the Second Epistle . . . to the Corinthians, *Works* (vol. 3), p.461; cf. the list of eleven evidences on pp. 472-475. Also, Geoffrey Nuttall, *The Holy Spirit in Puritan Faith and Experience*, p. 59.

16. Richard Sibbes, Bowels Opened, *Works* (vol. 2), p. 107; cf. p. 131; Soul's Conflict with Itself, *Works* (vol. 1), p. 194.

17. Richard Sibbes, Bowels Opened, *Works* (vol. 2), p. 103.

18. Richard Sibbes, Bruised Reed, *Works* (vol. 1), p. 50.

a danger in the human heart. The unity of Geneva and Westminster is striking on this point, and Sibbes is a faithful disciple of Calvin here. He continues, "Another cause of disquiet is, that men by a natural kind of popery seek for their comfort too much sanctification, neglecting justification, relying too much upon their own performances."[19] When corruption was so strong that one could see nothing of sanctification, the believer should remember that one's salvation did not come from assurance, and that, as Sibbes writes,

> God can see somewhat of his own Spirit in that confusion, but the spirit [of the believer] itself cannot. Then go to the blood of Christ! There is always comfort. … Go … to the blood of Christ, that is, if we find sin upon our consciences, if we find not peace in our consciences, nor sanctification in our hearts, go to the blood of Christ, which is shed for all those that confess their sins, and rely on him for pardon, though we find no grace; … before we go to Christ it is sufficient that we see nothing in ourselves, no qualification; for the graces of the Spirit they are not the condition of coming to Christ, but the promise of those that receive Christ after. Therefore go to Christ when thou feelest neither joy of the Spirit, nor sanctification of the Spirit; go to the blood of Christ, and that will purge thee, and wash thee from all thy sins.[20]

Though "the evidence indeed to prove our faith to be a true faith, is from works, … the title we have is only by

19. Richard Sibbes, Soul's Conflict with Itself, *Works* (vol. 1), p. 138.
20. Richard Sibbes, Learned Commentary . . . upon the First Chapter of the Second Epistle . . . to the Corinthians, *Works* (vol. 3), p. 464.

Christ, only by grace."[21] This was to be the ultimate basis of assurance for the Christian, as Sibbes taught: "We are more safe in his comprehending of us, than in our clasping and holding of him. As we say of the mother and the child, both hold, but the safety of the child is that the mother holds him."[22] Those people ten years later who worked on the *Directory* encouraged what Sibbes and so many others had already been doing: "In exhorting to duties, he is, as he seeth cause, to teach also the means that help to the performance of them."[23]

The Lord Jesus himself was very practical in His teachings, in His parables, and in His example. While He never taught people that they could save themselves, His last commission was plainly a call to teach people to obey all He had commanded. When we look to the apostles, we see the same blending of truth and application (for instance, see 1 Pet. 3).

In his essay, "Recovering the Plumb Line,"[24] Mike Horton writes,

> In law–gospel preaching, the believer is faced with his inability to satisfy God and God's solution to the problem in the person and work of Christ; in moralistic or 'practical' preaching, the believer is encouraged to satisfy God (or, as is more often the case, himself) by imitating the example of David, Solomon, Jesus, or Paul. The law is not as deadly and the gospel is not as free in this kind of preaching, and it

---

21. Richard Sibbes, The Faithful Covenanter, *Works* (vol. 6), p. 5.
22. Richard Sibbes, Bowels Opened, *Works* (vol. 2), p. 184.
23. see p. 96 of this book.
24. Michael Horton, "Recovering the Plumb Line," in *The Coming Evangelical Crisis*, ed., John Armstrong (Moody, 1996), p. 264.

leaves believers trusting a little in themselves and a little in God, and largely unsure of the nature of their hope. By recovering a diet of guilt, grace, and gratitude as the pillars of biblical preaching and teaching, we will be restoring the sufficiency of Scripture as "the power of God unto salvation" (KJV) in the pulpit and pew.

Those of us who are called to preach must remember that direct, practical application need not entail either moralism or works-salvation. In fact, our call to declare God's Word to God's people *includes* a call to practical application of scriptural truth.

Application must deal with sin fully
The Puritans urge preachers to consider the full ramifications of sin. While decrying sin, preachers must be especially careful to show the nature of sin, its importance, its effects, its danger for the hearers, remedies for it, and how best to avoid it.

The Puritans have left us rich legacies of such preaching and instruction. Examples include John Owen's *Mortification of Sin* and his *Indwelling Sin in Believers.* John Bunyan addressed the spreading nature of sin as he preached through Ephesians. Jonathan Edwards delivered penetrating sermons on charity and its fruits, and he commented that he thinks he saw more conversions while preaching on Romans 3:19 and the topic of men being "without excuse before God" than when preaching on any other text of Scripture.

This approach is supported in the *Directory*: "In dehortation, reprehension, and publick admonition (which require special wisdom), let him, as there shall be cause, not only discover the nature and greatness of the sin, with the misery attending it, but also show the danger his hearers are in to be overtaken and surprised by it, together with the remedies and best way to avoid it." "Dehortation, reprehension, and public admonition" are not words that are often heard in homiletics classrooms today. Nevertheless, they are an important component of biblical preaching.

Paul is doing the same thing in Romans 1-3. He is tracking down sin very particularly, but in no way is he denigrating grace. The more fully he traces out sin, the more Christ's love is magnified. Paul brings glory to God, in part, by laying out a fulsome denunciation of human sin, of our distorting God's image.

Contemporary preachers should also heed this injunction *not* to shy away from sin and judgment. It is true that preaching on sin and judgment can be done either well or poorly. But that is no excuse for avoiding it. There is no life driven by any true purpose which is not honest about sin. An understanding of sin can be the missing puzzle piece for many who understand little of God's nature. For instance, a woman who came to our church was raised as an agnostic. She had been brought up never to label anything as "wrong." But as she was researching a particular criminal, she came to the realization that what he had done was truly *wrong*. This was a turning point for her. Many others share her perspective – those in the world at large and even people in our churches. Preachers do them no favors by refusing to preach fully and clearly on sin. Life makes more sense even for unbelievers if they can understand that something is eternally and objectively *wrong*. The counsel of the Puritans, then, is wise counsel for those charged with preaching God's word.

Application should comfort fully

The Puritanical emphasis on sin and judgment is not without a corresponding message of salvation and mercy. The Puritans remind preachers to carefully apply comfort to those who are in need of it.

In his book *Preaching and Preachers*, D. Martyn Lloyd-Jones wrote,

> I shall never cease to be grateful to one [Puritan] ... called Richard Sibbes who was balm to my soul at a period in my life when I was overworked and badly overtired, and therefore subject in an unusual manner to the onslaughts of the devil. In that state and condition to read theology does not help, indeed it may be well-nigh impossible; what you need is some gentle, tender treatment for your soul. I found at that time that Richard Sibbes, who was known in London in the early seventeenth century as 'The Heavenly Doctor Sibbes' was an unfailing remedy. His books *The Bruised Reed* and *The Soul's Conflict with Itself* quietened, soothed, comforted, encouraged and healed me.[25]

Sibbes preached a series of sermons in London that later became one of his most well-known works, *The Bruised Reed & Smoking Flax*. He writes as follows:

"There is no more comfort to be expected from Christ, than there is care to please him."[26]

"For ... our encouragement to a thorough work of bruising, and patience under God's bruising of us, let all

25. D. Martyn Lloyd-Jones, *Preaching & Preachers*, Grand Rapids, 1972, p. 175
26. Richard Sibbes, Bruised Reed, *Works* (vol. 1), p.40.

know that none are fitter for comfort than those that think themselves furthest off."[27]

"...if there be any bruised reed, let him not except himself, when Christ doth not except him; 'Come unto me, all ye that are weary and heavy laden,' &c., Matthew 11:28.Why should we not make use of so gracious a disposition? We are only therefore poor, because we know not our riches in Christ. In time of temptation, rather believe Christ than the devil, believe truth from truth itself, hearken not to a liar, an enemy, and a murderer."[28]

"Whatsoever may be wished for in an all-sufficient comforter, is all to be found in Christ."[29]

"Such as take up a hope of their own, that Christ will suffer them to walk in the ways to hell, and yet bring them to heaven [offends deeply against this merciful disposition of Christ]: whereas all comfort should draw us nearer to Christ, else it is a lying comfort, either in itself or in our application of it."[30]

"the first and chief ground of our comfort is, that Christ as a priest offered himself as a sacrifice to his Father for us."[31]

"their [the apostles'] comforts grew with their troubles..."[32]

---

27. Ibid. I.48.
28. Ibid. I.70
29. Ibid. I.73
30. Ibid. I.73
31. Ibid. I.79
32. Ibid. I.94

"O beloved, it is a comfortable thing to conceive of Christ aright, to know what love, mercy, strength we have laid up for us in the breast of Christ. A good conceit of the physician, we say, is half the cure; let us make use of this his mercy and power every day, in our daily combats.... Christ will not leave us, till he hath made us like himself.... What a comfort is this in our conflicts with our unruly hearts, that it shall not always be thus! Let us strive a little while, and we shall be happy for ever. Let us think when we are troubled with our sins, that Christ hath this in charge of his Father, 'that he shall not quench the smoking flax,' until he hath subdued all. This putteth a shield into our hands to beat back all 'the fiery darts of Satan,' Ephesians 6:16. He will object, (1.) thou art a great sinner; we may answer, Christ is a strong Saviour; but he will object, (2.) thou hast no faith, no love; yes, a spark of faith and love; but (3.) Christ will not regard that; yes, 'he will not quench the smoking flax;' but (4.) this is so little and weak, that it will vanish and come to nought: nay, but Christ will cherish it, until he hath brought judgment to victory."[33]

In none of this was Sibbes out of step with the understanding of the Assembly that was to be convened a few years after his home-going. The *Directory* reads: "In applying comfort, whether general against all temptations, or particular against some special troubles or terrors, he is carefully to *answer* such objections as a troubled heart and afflicted spirit may suggest to the contrary." [emphasis mine]

Here, too, the Divines were faithful to Scripture. Following his resurrection, Jesus was very careful to speak

---

33. Ibid. I.98

honestly and yet comfortingly to Peter. Likewise, Barnabas was careful and encouraging to Paul, and more tender than the great apostle with Mark. Paul himself wrote in Galatians 6:1 of the need to restore gently those caught in sin. Furthermore, Hebrews, I Peter, and Revelation are among several entire books of the New Testament which are meant, in substantial parts, to offer encouragement to afflicted Christians.

The great consolation of hope must not be overlooked. Hope comforts fully, the kind of hope offered in Hebrews 10–11. As we see at the end of Romans 8, a God who has given us His only Son, "how will he not also, along with him, graciously give us all things?" (Rom. 8:32). Preachers must not be scared off into being mundane, practical secularists, neither by yesterday's materialists nor by today's realized eschatology communitarians. Both groups are in serious error and departure from the Reformed tradition when they steal away the hope of heaven from those who hold it dear. When "kingdom-centered" is used to effectively oppose "heavenly-minded," then you know that the kingdom such critics are representing is not the kingdom of God! The ἐπουρανίου [heavenly] kingdom that we desire is, as Paul says in 2 Timothy 4:18, the one that God will bring him to safely. The ἐπουρανίου [heavenly] city that we desire is, as we read in Hebrews 11:16, a better one, prepared by God, for us. Paul could not be more clear than he is in 1 Corinthians 15:19 that if we have hope only for this life, then we are of all men most to be pitied. When preachers fail to highlight this hope, they rob listeners of the comfort God has for them in his word.

Application should cause self-examination

Sermons should help the hearers examine themselves. To contemporary ears, this proposition may seem objectionable. Yet a closer reading of the Puritans reveals an important point. In his farewell sermon of August 1662, Edmund Calamy said at one point, on sin and prosperity:

> May be some will say, I have committed many ... sins, but am not brought into any [difficulty]. Remember, it was nine months after David had numbered the people before he was in [his difficulty]; but as sure as God is in heaven, sin will bring [difficulties] sooner or later; though one sin a hundred years, yet shall he be accursed; may be thy prosperity makes way for thy damnation; and this is thy greatest distress, **that thou goest on in sin and prosperity**.[34] (emphasis mine).

This was his final word to the congregation that he was leaving. The *Westminster Directory* states,

> It is also sometimes requisite to give some notes of trial (which is very profitable, especially when performed by able and experienced ministers, with circumspection and prudence, and the signs clearly grounded on the holy scripture), whereby the hearers may be able to **examine themselves** whether they have attained those graces, and performed those duties, to which he exhorteth, or be guilty of the sin reprehended, and in danger of the judgements threatened, or are such to whom the consolations

---

34. Edmund Calamy in his *Farewell Sermons* Reprint Sola Deo Gloria Publishers, 1992. (originally published 1662), p. 11.

propounded do belong; that accordingly they may be quickened and excited to duty, humbled for their wants and sins, affected with their danger, and strengthened with comfort, as their condition, upon examination, shall require.[35]

That such trying sermons are biblical should be beyond question. Paul calls for the most serious self-examination in 1 Corinthians 6 and 11, and Peter does the same in 2 Peter 1. Many other examples from the Scriptures could be cited.

Applying this principle today, preachers must not think only in terms of their listeners. Sermons are not just focused on "those bad people out there," or "those unsaved people," but on the very ones who preach the Word! Preachers need the gospel just as everyone else does. Preachers need the free, sheer grace of God as much in the present as they did the first time they heard it. In light of continuing sin after knowing God's grace, preachers need it even more! This same principle is true for those who hear them. A call to self-examination is also a call to accept God's grace. Graciously owned self-examination will always lead to "cross"-examination.

Application should relate to helpful doctrines drawn from the text
A given text may address multiple doctrines, but the Puritans admonish preachers to choose those doctrines which are most helpful to the hearers. The applications that spring from sermons based on helpful doctrines will yield more and better fruit among the hearers.

William Gouge preached very particularly from Ephesians 5 and 6 about the duties of wives and husbands, of children and parents, of servants and masters. And

---

35. See p. 96 of this book

William Gurnall's *Christian in Complete Armour,* preached to his hearers in the wool town of Lavenham, Suffolk, was preached for their particular spiritual benefit.

The *Directory* says, "And, as he needeth not always to prosecute every doctrine which lies in his text, so is he wisely to make choice of such uses, as by his residence and conversing with his flock, he findeth most needful and seasonable; and, amongst these, such as may most draw their souls to Christ, the fountain of light, holiness and comfort."[36]

In this, the Divines were following the model they saw in the occasional letters in the New Testament. Was not Paul choosing to preach certain doctrines that he knew would be particularly helpful for his readers/hearers in Galatians, and in 1 & 2 Corinthians? Does not Peter do this in 1 Peter?

Today, preachers should acknowledge that the same text can be preached both correctly and yet differently at various times and in diverse settings. While the truths preached should be timeless, they should be presented in the garb of the times and places in which we live.

The Puritans on Preaching: Method

In addition to controversy and application, the Puritans set forth guidelines about homiletic method. Although the Puritans have often been criticized on the basis of their methods in preaching, these preachers actually made very balanced observations about how preachers should go about their task. Those who hear and heed their advice are bound to profit from it. In sum, they believed that some aspects of preaching are variable, while others must always remain the same.

---

36. See p. 97 of this book.

Variable elements of preaching

The Puritans said that preaching can be accomplished in different ways. Such variation in method is not required, but can be helpful. It follows from this that not everyone should preach the same way. Different preachers may adopt varying methods depending upon their gifts and the congregation's needs.

Some Puritan preachers were known more for teaching, such as Owen and Edwards, while others were known for exhorting, such as Bunyan and Whitefield. Both kinds of preachers are essential to the work of the kingdom. God gives varying gifts to be used for the good of His people.

As the *Westminster Directory* puts it, "This method is not prescribed as necessary for every man, or upon every text; but only recommended, as being found by experience to be very much blessed of God, and very helpful for the people's understandings and memories.…Where there are more ministers in a congregation than one, and they of different gifts, each may more especially apply himself to doctrine or exhortation, according to the gift wherein he most excelleth, and as they shall agree between themselves."[37]

You can almost hear echoes of the converted fisherman Peter's comment about the converted Pharisee Paul in 2 Peter 3:15, when he says of him "our dear brother Paul also wrote you with the wisdom that God gave him. He writes the same way in all his letters, speaking in them of these matters. His letters contain some things that are hard to understand, which ignorant and unstable people distort.…" Perhaps Paul was a Presbyterian and Peter was a Baptist! But they each understood that some differences are of more significance than others.

---

37. See p. 97 & 99

Preachers must therefore be careful not to make essential some means simply because they have seen God bless it in their own ministry. When pastors see a measure of growth or success in their congregations, they must pray, "Oh God, deliver us from being men whose small success make us largely unteachable." If God is big enough to use one preacher, he can probably use another one down the road. Preachers can model this belief by honoring other staff members or guest preachers, by praying for other local evangelical churches, and above all, by training people to supremely love the God who is preached rather than the man who is preaching.

Invariable elements of preaching
Although some aspects of preaching may vary from good sermon to good sermon or from good preacher to good preacher, the Puritans maintained that all preaching should require certain methods. They expressed this by means of seven adverbs that describe how preaching should be done: painfully, plainly, faithfully, wisely, gravely, lovingly, and earnestly.

1)Painfully:
On first glance, this may seem an odd description. By advocating "painful" preaching, the Puritans refer to the practice of "taking pains" in preparation and presentation; they urge preachers not to treat their responsibilities casually. The *Directory* describes this as laboring "painfully, not doing the work of the Lord negligently." Painfully preparing, Thomas Manton would often transcribe his sermons more than once, sometimes sitting up all Saturday night re-writing them. He would get up during the night if he had a good thought, and write for an hour. Certainly John

Knowles, Congregational preacher in London, fulfilled the ideal of painful presentation. "It is said of him that sometimes while preaching, his very earnestness and zeal so exhausted him that he fainted and fell,"[38] that "he was so fervent in his work, that he sometimes preached till he [literally] fell down." This is an expression of one man's experience and need not be viewed as the norm. However, the point is clear and should not be ignored.

2)*Plainly*:

As Thomas Goodwin's son records in his memoir of his father, when Goodwin had come to Cambridge he found "the plain and earnest manner of the Puritan preachers of Cambridge ... distasteful to him.... The preaching he admired was that of Dr Senhouse," who was later to preach the coronation sermon for Charles I in 1626, "distinguished rather for its ostentatious display of rhetoric than for its clear statement of evangelical truth.... He was especially ambitious of becoming an eloquent and popular, rather than an evangelical and useful preacher." Throughout his early university career, "the prevalent desire of his heart was to be distinguished as a popular, learned, and eloquent preacher, 'like the great wits of St. Mary's, who strove to exceed each other in a vain-glorious eloquence.' While such preaching was the object of his laborious imitation, it afforded no satisfaction to his conscience or his heart."[39] And when he was converted, Goodwin turned to the kind of preaching he heard from Sibbes, John Preston, and others–preaching that was plain and clear to all.

---

38. "Knowles, John," in *Cyclopedia of Biblical, Theological, and Ecclesiastical Literature,* eds., John McClintock and James Strong, vol.V K-Mc (prt. Baker Book House, 1981), p. 137

39. Thomas Goodwin, Jr. Memoir of Dr. Thomas Goodwin, in *The Works of Thomas Goodwin*, vol.2, Edinburgh, 1861, p. 15

The *Directory* admonishes that preachers preach "Plainly, that the meanest may understand; delivering the truth not in the enticing words of man's wisdom, but in demonstration of the Spirit and of power, lest the cross of Christ should be made of none effect; abstaining also from an unprofitable use of unknown tongues, strange phrases, and cadences of sounds and words; sparingly citing sentences of ecclesiastical or other human writer, ancient or modern, be they never so elegant."[40]

The touching story of Dr. Manton, lecturing before the Lord Mayor of London, further exemplifies the role of clarity in good preaching.

Being about to preach before the Lord Mayor, the court of Aldermen, &c. at St. Paul's, Doctor Thomas Manton chose a subject in which he had an opportunity of displaying his judgment and learning. He was heard with admiration and applause by the more intelligent part of the audience; but as he was returning from dinner with the Lord Mayor in the evening, a poor man following him, pulled him by the sleeve of his gown, and asked him if he were the gentleman that preached before the Lord Mayor. He replied, he was. 'Sir,' said he, "I came with hopes of getting some good to my soul, but I was greatly disappointed, for I could not understand a great deal of what you said; you were quite above me.' The Doctor replied with tears 'Friend, if I did not give you a sermon, you have given me one, and by the grace of God, I will never play the fool to preach before my Lord Mayor in such a manner again.'[41]

---

40. See pp. 97 of this book.

3)Faithfully & Wisely:

According to the *Directory*, preachers must work "*faithfully*, looking at the honor of Christ, the conversion, edification, and salvation of the people, not at his own gain or glory; keeping nothing back which may promote those holy ends, giving to every one his own portion, and bearing indifferent respect unto all, without neglecting the meanest, or sparing the greatest in their sins. *Wisely*, framing all his doctrines, exhortations, and especially his reproofs, in such a manner as may be most likely to prevail; showing all due respect to each man's person and place, and not mixing his own passion or bitterness" [emphasis mine].[42]

4)Gravely:

As Richard Baxter wrote in his *Love Breathing Thanks and Praise*, "I preach'd as never sure to preach again, And as a dying man to dying men!"[43] The *Westminster Directory* phrases it as follows: "Gravely, as becometh the Word of God; shunning all such gesture, voice, and expressions, as may occasion the corruptions of men to despise him and his ministry."[44] Much more could be said in application of this point, but for preachers who are interested, I would recommend Spurgeon's *Lectures to My Students*, or a conversation with one's residential homiletics professor – one's spouse!

5)Lovingly:

Examples of loving preaching include Sibbes' care as evidenced in quotes above, or Baxter's pastoral passion. The *Directory* notes that the preacher is always to preach "With

---

41. (Palmer I. 140) recounted by William Harris, repeated in intro to *Farewell Sermons*.

42. See p. 97-98 of this book

43. Richard Baxter, *Poetical Fragments*, 2nd Ed., London, 1689 p. 30

44. See p. 99 of this book

loving affection, that the people may see **all** coming from his godly zeal, and hearty desire to do them good."[45]

6)Earnestly:
Thomas Goodwin told the story of how when he was an undergraduate at Cambridge,

"having heard much of Mr. Rogers of Dedham took a journey ... to hear him preach.... Mr. Rogers was ... on the subject of ... the Scriptures. And in that sermon he falls into an expostulation with the people telling about their neglect of the Bible; ... he personates God to the people, telling them, 'Well, I have trusted you so long with my Bible; you have slighted it, it lies in such and such houses all covered with dust and cobwebs; you care not to listen to it. Do you use my Bible so? Well, you shall have my Bible no longer.' And he takes up the Bible from his cushion, and seemed as if he were going away with it and carrying it from them; but immediately turns again and personates the people to God, falls down on his knees, cries and pleads most earnestly, 'Lord, whatever thou dost to us, take not thy Bible from us; kill our children, burn our houses, destroy our goods; only spare us thy Bible, only take not away thy Bible.' And then he personates God again to the peoples: 'Say you so? Well, I will try you a while longer; and here is my Bible for you. I will see how you will use it, whether you will love it more ... observe it more ... practice it more, and live more according to it.' By these actions ... he put all the congregation into so strange a posture that ... the people generally ... [were] deluged with their own tears; and he told

45. See p. 99 of this book

me that he himself, when he got out … was fain to hang a quarter of an hour upon the neck of his horse weeping before he had power to mount; so strange an impression was there upon him, and generally upon the people, upon having been expostulated with for the neglect of the Bible."[46]

The *Directory* stipulates that the preacher is to preach "As taught of God, and persuaded in his own heart, that all that he teacheth is the truth of Christ; and walking before his flock, as an example to them in it; earnestly, both in private and publick, recommending his labours to the blessing of God, and watchfully looking to himself, and the flock whereof the Lord hath made him overseer: So shall the doctrine of truth be preserved uncorrupt, many souls converted and built up, and himself receive manifold comforts of his labours even in this life, and afterward the crown of glory laid up for him in the world to come."

Such preaching should be expected from those who have the qualities listed for elders in 1 Timothy and Titus. As Paul said to the Corinthians, preaching is not shaped fundamentally by earthly wisdom. And so, we're back to where we began with preaching, taking it *so* seriously, because it is *so* important.

Conclusion

What I have done here is simply to restate key principles from *The Westminster Directory for the Publick Worship of* God, giving them contemporary garb by using Puritan illustrations, scripture proofs, and potential applications. I urge you to reflect on the *Directory's* text as I have done, seeking

---

46. Thomas Goodwin, Jr. Memoir of Dr. Thomas Goodwin, in *The Works of Thomas Goodwin*, vol.2 (James Nichol; Edinburgh, 1861) p. 17-18.

edification and clarification concerning the art of preaching. God has deigned to use preachers to be the heralds of life, to be the instruments to gather his flock to himself, and preaching is a subject that is eminently worthy of our attention. As a final word, I offer the story of Hugh Peters, a man whom many have never heard of, but who certainly exhibits a passion for preaching that we would all be privileged to share.

Born in 1598 in Cornwall in England, Peters was educated at Cambridge. He was converted at age 22 while hearing a sermon at St. Paul's, London. He was deeply struck with a sense of sin. Thereafter, he lived and preached in Essex. During the 1620's, he became a popular preacher at one of the churches in London. Because he had questions of conscience about some of the things his bishop was requiring him to do, he was silenced for non-conformity and actually imprisoned. He escaped England, and for a few years preached in Holland, and then in New England, where his wife died. In the 1640's he returned to England, and got caught up in the struggles of the English Civil war on the side of the Parliament. A kind man, personally, he became very popular, and very active in affairs of state. While his health was declining in his early 60's, the government changed, and Charles II came to reclaim the English throne. Peters was immediately arrested and imprisoned in the Tower for complicity in Charles I's execution (a fair charge). A month later he was convicted of high treason. And what did this kindly, ailing, spent man do just two days before his own execution? He got permission to preach to the other prisoners, and to anyone else who would hear him preach in Newgate prison where he was held. He, too, preached as a dying man to dying men.

The Directory
For
The Publick Worship
of
God

The Directory

for

The Publick Worship of God

CHARLES I. Parl. 3. Sess. 5.
*An ACT of the PARLIAMENT of the KINGDOM
of SCOTLAND, approving and establishing the
DIRECTORY for Publick Worship.*

AT EDINBURGH, February 6, 1645.

THE Estates of Parliament now convened, in the second session of this first triennial Parliament, by virtue of the last act of the last Parliament holden by his Majesty and the Three Estates, in anno 1641; after the publick reading and serious consideration of the act under-written of the General Assembly, approving the following Directory for the publick worship of God in the three kingdoms, lately united by the Solemn League and Covenant, together with the ordinance of the Parliament of England establishing the said Directory, and the Directory itself; do heartily and cheerfully agree to the said Directory, according to the act of the General Assembly approving the same. Which act, together with the Directory it-self; the Estates of Parliament do, without a contrary voice, ratify and approve in all the Heads and Articles thereof; and do interpone and add the authority of Parliament to the said act of the General Assembly. And do ordain the same to have the strength and force of a law and act of parliament, and execution to pass thereupon, for observing the said Directory, according to the said act of the General Assembly to al points.

Alex. Gibson, *Cler. Registri.*

ASSEMBLY AT EDINBURGH,
February 3, 1645, Sess. 10.

*ACT of the GENERAL ASSEMBLY
of the KIRK of SCOTLAND, for the
establishing and putting in Execution of the
DIRECTORY for the
Publick Worship of God.*

Whereas an happy unity, and uniformity in religion amongst the kirks of Christ, in these three kingdoms, united under one Sovereign, having been long and earnestly wished for by the godly and well-affected amongst us, was propounded as a main article of the large treaty, without which band and bulwark, no safe, well-grounded, and lasting peace could be expected; and afterward, with greater strength and maturity, revived in the Solemn League and Covenant of the three kingdoms; whereby they stand straitly obliged to endeavour the nearest uniformity in one form of Church government, Directory of Worship, Confession of Faith, and Form of Catechising; which hath also before, and since our entering into that Covenant, been the matter of many supplications and remonstrances, and sending Commissioners to the King's Majesty; of declarations to the Honourable Houses of the Parliament of England, and of letters to the Reverend Assembly of Divines, and others of the ministry of the kirk of England; being also the end of our sending Commissioners, as was desired, from this kirk, with commission to treat of uniformity in the four particulars afore-mentioned, with such committees as should be appointed by both Houses of Parliament of England, and by the Assembly of Divines sitting at Westminster; and beside all this, it being, in point of conscience, the chief motive and end of our adventuring upon manifold and great hazards, for quenching the devouring flame of the present unnatural and bloody war in England, thought of the weakening of this kingdom within itself, and the advantage of the enemy which have invaded it; accounting nothing too dear to us, so that this our joy be fulfilled. And now this great work being so far advanced, that a Directory for the Publick Worship of God in all the three kingdoms being agreed upon by the Honourable Houses of the parliament of England, after consultation with the Divines of both kingdoms there assembled, and sent to us for our approbation, that, being also agreed upon by this kirk and kingdom of Scotland, it may be in the name of both kingdoms presented to the King, for his royal consent and ratification; the General Assembly, having most seriously considered, revised, and examined the Directory afore-mentioned, after several publick readings of it, after much deliberation, both publickly and in private committees, after full liberty given to all to object against it, and earnest invitations of all who have any scruples about it, to make known the same, that they might be satisfied; doth unanimously, and without a contrary voice, agree to and approve the following Directory, in all the heads thereof, together with the Preface set before it; and doth require, decern, and ordain, That, according to the plain tenor and meaning thereof, and the intent of the Preface, it be carefully and uniformly observed and practised by all the ministers and others within this kingdom whom it doth concern; which practice shall be begun, upon intimation given to the several presbyteries from the printing of this Directory, that a printed copy of it be provided and kept for the use of every kirk in this kingdom; also that each presbytery have a printed copy thereof for their use, and take special notice of the observation or neglect thereof in every General Assembly, as there shall be cause. Provided always, That the clause in the Directory, of the administration of the Lord's Supper, which mentioneth the communicants sitting about the table, or at it, be not interpreted as if, in the judgment of this kirk, it were indifferent, and free for any of the communicants not to come to, and receive at the table; or as if we did approve the distributing of the elements by the minister to each communicant, and not by the communicants among themselves. It is also provided, That this shall be no prejudice to the order and practise of this kirk, in such particulars as are appointed by the books of discipline, and acts of General Assemblies, as are not otherwise ordered and appointed in the Directory.

Finally, The Assembly doth, with much joy and thankfulness, acknowledge the rich blessing and invaluable mercy of God, in bringing the so much wished for uniformity in religion to such a happy period, that these kingdoms, once at so great a distance in the form of worship, are now, by the blessing of God brought to a nearer uniformity than any other reformed kirks; which is unto us the return of our prayers, and lightening of our eyes, and reviving of our hearts in the midst our many sorrows and sufferings; a taking away, in great measure, the reproach of the people of God, to the stopping of the mouths of malignant and disaffected persons; and an opening of the door of hope, that God hath yet thoughts of peace towards us, and not of evil, to give us an expected end; in the expectation an confidence whereof we do rejoice; beseeching the Lord to preserve these kingdoms from heresies, schisms, offences, profaneness, and whatsoever is contrary to sound doctrine, and the power of godliness; and to continue with us, and the generations following, these his pure and purged ordinances, together with an increase of the power and life thereof, to the glory of his great name, the enlargement of the kingdom of his Son, the corroboration of peace and love between the kingdoms, the unity and comfort of all his people, and our edifying one another in love.

THE PREFACE

IN the beginning of the blessed Reformation, our wise and pious ancestors took care to set forth an order for redress of many things, which they then, by the word, discovered to be vain, erroneous, superstitious, and idolatrous, in the publick worship of God. This occasioned many godly and learned men to rejoice much in the Book of Common Prayer, at that time set forth; because the mass, and the rest of the Latin service being removed, the publick worship was celebrated in our own tongue: many of the common people also receive benefit by hearing the scriptures read in their own language, which formerly were unto them as a book that is sealed.

Howbeit, long and sad experience hath made it manifest, that the Liturgy used in the Church of England, (notwithstanding all the pains and religious intentions of the Compilers of it,) hath proved an offence, not only to many of the godly at home, but also to the reformed Churches abroad. For, not to speak of urging the reading of all the prayers, which very greatly increased the burden of it, the many unprofitable and burdensome ceremonies contained in it have occasioned much mischief, as well by disquieting the consciences of many godly ministers and people, who could not yield unto them, as by depriving them of the ordinances of God, which they might not enjoy without conforming or subscribing to those ceremonies. Sundry good Christians have been, by means thereof, kept from the Lord's table; and divers able and faithful ministers debarred from the exercise of their ministry, (to the endangering of many thousand souls, in a time of such scarcity of faithful pastors,) and spoiled of their livelihood, to the undoing of them and their families. Prelates, and their faction, have laboured to raise the estimation of it to such a height, as if there were no other worship, or way of worship of God, amongst us, but only the Service-book; to the great hinderance of the preaching of the word, and (in some places, especially of late) to the justling of it out as unnecessary, or at best, as far inferior to the reading of common prayer; which was made no better than an idol by many ignorant and superstitious people, who, pleasing themselves in their presence at that service, and their lip-labour in bearing a part in it, have thereby hardened themselves in their ignorance and carelessness of saving knowledge and true piety.

In the meantime, Papists boasted that the book was a compliance with them in a great part of their service; and so were not a little confirmed in their superstition and idolatry, expecting rather our return to them, than endeavouring the reformation of themselves: in which expectation they were of late very much encouraged, when, upon the pretended warrantableness of imposing of the former ceremonies, new ones were daily obtruded upon the Church.

Add hereunto, (which was not foreseen, but since have come to pass,) that the Liturgy hath been a great means, as on the one hand to make and increase an idle and unedifying ministry, which contented itself with set forms made to their hands by others, without putting forth themselves to exercise the gift of prayer, with which our Lord Jesus Christ pleaseth to furnish all his servants whom he calls to that office: so, on the other side, it hath been (and ever

would be, if continued) a matter of endless strife and con-
tention in the Church, and a snare both to many godly and
faithful ministers, who have been persecuted and silenced
upon that occasion, and to others of hopeful parts, many of
which have been, and more still would be, diverted from
all thoughts of the ministry to other studies; especially in
these latter times, wherein God vouchsafeth to his people
more and better means for the discovery of error and superstition, and for attaining of knowledge in the mysteries
of godliness, and gifts in preaching and prayer.

Upon these, and many the like weighty considerations
in reference to the whole book in general, and because
of divers particulars contained in it; not from any love
to novelty, or intention to disparage our first reformers,
(of whom we are persuaded, that, were they now alive,
they would join with us in this work, and whom we
acknowledge as excellent instruments, raised by God, to
begin the purging and building of his house, and desire they
may be had of us and posterity in everlasting remembrance,
with thankfulness and honour,) but that we may in some
measure answer the gracious providence of God, which at
this time calleth upon us for further reformation, and may
satisfy our own consciences, and answer the expectation
of other reformed churches, and the desires of many of
the godly among ourselves, and withal give some publick
testimony of our endeavours for uniformity in divine
worship, which we have promised in our Solemn League
and Covenant; we have, after earnest and frequent calling
upon the name of God, and after much consultation, not
with flesh and blood, but with his holy word, resolved
to lay aside the former Liturgy, with the many rites and
ceremonies formerly used in the worship of God; and

have agreed upon this following Directory for all the parts of publick worship, at ordinary and extraordinary times. Wherein our care hath been to hold forth such things as are of divine institution in every ordinance; and other things we have endeavoured to set forth according to the rules of Christian prudence, agreeable to the general rules of the word of God; our meaning therein being only, that the general heads, the sense and scope of the prayers, and other parts of publick worship, being known to all, there may be a consent of all the churches in those things that contain the substance of the service and worship of God; and the ministers may be hereby directed, in their administrations, to keep like soundness in doctrine and prayer, and may, if need be, have some help and furniture, and yet so as they become not hereby slothful and negligent in stirring up the gifts of Christ in them; but that each one, by meditation, by taking heed to himself, and the flock of God committed to him, and by wise observing the ways of Divine Providence, may be careful to furnish his heart and tongue with further or other materials of prayer and exhortation, as shall be needful upon all occasions.

OF THE ASSEMBLING OF THE CONGREGATION, AND THEIR BEHAVIOUR IN THE PUBLICK WORSHIP OF GOD

When the congregation is to meet for publick worship, the people (having before prepared their hearts thereunto) ought all to come and join therein; not absenting themselves from the publick ordinance through negligence, or upon pretence of private meetings.

Let all enter the assembly, not irreverently, but in a grave and seemly manner, taking their seats or places without adoration, or bowing themselves towards one place or other.

The congregation being assembled, the minister, after solemn calling on them to the worshipping of the great name of God, is to begin with prayer.

"In all reverence and humility acknowledging the incomprehensible greatness and majesty of the Lord, (in whose presence they do then in a special manner appear,) and their own vileness and unworthiness to approach so near him, with their utter inability of themselves to so great a work; and humbly beseeching him for pardon, assistance, and acceptance, in the whole service then to be performed; and for a blessing on that particular portion of his word then to be read: And all in the name and mediation of the Lord Jesus Christ."

The publick worship being begun, the people are wholly to attend upon it, forbearing to read any thing, except what the minister is then reading or citing; and abstaining much more from all private whisperings, conferences, salutations, or doing reverence to any person present, or coming in; as also from all gazing, sleeping, and other indecent behaviour, which may disturb the minister or people, or hinder themselves or others in the service of God.

If any, through necessity, be hindered from being present at the beginning, they ought not, when they come into the congregation, to betake themselves to their private devotions, but reverently to compose themselves to join with the assembly in that ordinance of God which is then in hand.

OF PUBLICK READING
OF
THE HOLY SCRIPTURES

Reading of the word in the congregation, being part of the publick worship of God, (wherein we acknowledge our dependence upon him, and subjection to him,) and one mean sanctified by him for the edifying of his people, is to be performed by the pastors and teachers.

Howbeit, such as intend the ministry, may occasionally both read the word, and exercise their gift in preaching in the congregation, if allowed by the presbytery thereunto.

All the canonical books of the Old and New Testament (but none of those which are commonly called *Apocrypha*) shall be publickly read in the vulgar tongue, out of the best allowed translation, distinctly, that all may hear and understand.

How large a portion shall be read at once, is left to the wisdom of the minister; but it is convenient, that ordinarily one chapter of each Testament be read at every meeting; and sometimes more, where the chapters be short, or the coherence of matter requireth it.

It is requisite that all the canonical books be read over in order, that the people may be better acquainted with the whole body of the scriptures; and ordinarily, where the reading in either Testament endeth on one Lord's day, it is to begin the next.

We commend also the more frequent reading of such scriptures as he that readeth shall think best for edification of his hearers, as the book of Psalms, and such like.

When the minister who readeth shall judge it necessary to expound any part of what is read, let it not be done until the whole chapter or psalm be ended; and regard is always to be had unto the time, that neither preaching, nor other ordinances be straitened, or rendered tedious. Which rule is to be observed in all other publick performances.

Beside publick reading of the holy scriptures, every person that can read, is to be exhorted to read the scriptures privately, (and all others that cannot read, if not disabled by age, or otherwise, are likewise to be exhorted to learn to read,) and to have a Bible.

OF PUBLICK PRAYER
BEFORE THE SERMON

After reading of the word, (and singing of the psalm,) the minister who is to preach, is to endeavour to get his own and his hearers hearts to be rightly affected with their sins, that they may all mourn in sense thereof before the Lord, and hunger and thirst after the grace of God in Jesus Christ, by proceeding to a more full confession of sin, with shame and holy confusion of face, and to call upon the Lord to this effect:

"To acknowledge our great sinfulness, First, by reason of original sin, which (beside the guilt that makes us liable to everlasting damnation) is the seed of all other sins, hath depraved and poisoned all the faculties and powers of soul and body, doth defile our best actions, and (were it not restrained, or our hearts renewed by grace) would break forth into innumerable transgressions, and greatest rebellions against the Lord that ever were committed by the vilest of the sons of men; and next, by reason of actual sins, our own sins, the sins of magistrates, of ministers, and of the whole nation, unto which we are many ways accessory: which sins of ours receive many fearful aggravations, we having broken all the commandments of the holy, just, and good law of God, doing that which is forbidden, and leaving undone what is enjoined; and that not only out of ignorance and infirmity, but also more presumptuously, against the light of our minds, checks of our consciences, and motions of his own Holy Spirit to the contrary, so that we have no cloak for our sins; yea, not only despising the riches of God's goodness, forbearance, and long-suffering, but standing out against many invitations and offers of grace in the gospel;

not endeavouring, as we ought, to receive Christ into our hearts by faith, or to walk worthy of him in our lives.

To bewail our blindness of mind, hardness of heart, unbelief, impenitency, security, lukewarmness, barrenness; or not endeavouring after mortification and newness of life, nor after the exercise of godliness in the power thereof; and that the best of us have not so stedfastly walked with God, kept our garments so unspotted, nor been so zealous of his glory, and the good of others, as we ought: and to mourn over such other sins as the congregation is particularly guilty of, notwithstanding the manifold and great mercies of our God, the love of Christ, the light of the gospel, and reformation of religion, our own purposes, promises, vows, solemn covenant, and other special obligations, to the contrary.

To acknowledge and confess, that, as we are convinced of our guilt, so, out of a deep sense thereof, we judge ourselves unworthy of the smallest benefits, most worthy of God's fiercest wrath, and of all the curses of the law, and heaviest judgments inflicted upon the most rebellious sinners; and that he might most justly take his kingdom and gospel from us, plague us with all sorts of spiritual and temporal judgments in this life, and after cast us into utter darkness, in the lake that burneth with fire and brimstone, where is weeping and gnashing of teeth for evermore.

Notwithstanding all which, to draw near to the throne of grace, encouraging ourselves with hope of a gracious answer of our prayers, in the riches and all-sufficiency of that only one oblation, the satisfaction and intercession of the Lord Jesus Christ, at the right hand of his Father and our Father; and in confidence of the exceeding great and precious promises of mercy and grace in the new covenant, through the same Mediator thereof, to deprecate the heavy wrath and curse of God, which we are not able to avoid, or bear; and humbly and earnestly to supplicate for mercy, in the free and full remission of all our sins, and that only for the bitter sufferings and precious merits of that our only Saviour Jesus Christ.

That the Lord would vouchsafe to shed abroad his love in our hearts by the Holy Ghost; seal unto us, by the same Spirit of adoption, the full assurance of our pardon and reconciliation; comfort all that mourn in Zion, speak peace to the wounded and troubled spirit, and bind up the broken-hearted: and as for secure and presumptuous sinners, that he would open their eyes, convince their consciences, and turn them from darkness unto light, and from the power of Satan unto God, that they also may receive forgiveness of sin, and an inheritance among them that are sanctified by faith in Christ Jesus.

With remission of sins through the blood of Christ, to pray for sanctification by his Spirit; the mortification of sin dwelling in and many times tyrannizing over us; the quickening of our dead spirits with the life of God in Christ; grace to fit and enable us for all duties of conversation and callings towards God and men; strength against temptations; the sanctified use of blessings and crosses; and perseverance in faith and obedience unto the end.

To pray for the propagation of the gospel and kingdom of Christ to all nations; for the conversion of the Jews, the fulness of the Gentiles, the fall of Antichrist, and the hastening of the second coming of our Lord; for the deliverance of the distressed churches abroad from the tyranny of the antichristian faction, and from the cruel oppressions and blasphemies of the Turk; for the blessing of God upon the reformed churches, especially upon the churches and kingdoms of Scotland, England, and Ireland, now more strictly and religiously united in the Solemn National League and Covenant; and for our plantations in the remote parts of the world: more particularly for that church and kingdom whereof we are members, that therein God would establish peace and truth , the purity of all his ordinances, and the power of godliness; prevent and remove heresy, schism, profaneness, superstition, security, and unfruitfulness under the means of grace; heal all our rents and divisions, and preserve us from breach of our Solemn Covenant.

To pray for all in authority, especially for the King's Majesty; that God would make him rich in blessings, both in his person and government; establish his throne in religion and righteousness, save him from evil counsel, and make him a blessed and glorious instrument for the conservation and propagation of the gospel, for the encouragement and protection of them that do well, the terror of all that do evil, and the great good of the whole church, and of all his kingdoms; for the conversion of the Queen, the religious education of the Prince, and the rest of the royal seed; for the comforting of the afflicted Queen of Bohemia, sister to our Sovereign; and for the restitution and establishment of the illustrious Prince Charles, Elector Palatine of the Rhine, to all his dominions and dignities; for a blessing upon the High Court of Parliament, (when sitting in any of these kingdoms respectively,) the nobility, the subordinate judges and magistrates, the gentry, and all the commonality; for all pastors and teachers, that God would fill them with his Spirit, make them exemplarily holy, sober, just, peaceable, and gracious in their lives; sound, faithful, and powerful in their ministry; and follow all their labours with abundance of success and blessing; and give unto all his people pastors according to his own heart; for the universities, and all schools and religious seminaries of church and commonwealth, that they may flourish more and more in learning and piety; for the particular city or congregation, that God would pour out a blessing upon the ministry of the word, sacraments, and discipline, upon the civil government, and all the several families and persons therein; for mercy to the afflicted under any inward or outward distress; for seasonable weather, and fruitful seasons, as the time may require; for averting the judgments that we either feel or fear, or are liable unto as famine, pestilence, the sword, and such like.

And, with confidence of his mercy to his whole church, and the acceptance of our persons, through the merits and mediation of our High Priest, the Lord Jesus, to profess that it is the desire of our souls to have fellowship with God in the reverend and conscionable use of his holy ordinances; and, to that purpose, to pray earnestly for his grace and effectual assistance to the sanctification of his holy sabbath, the Lord's day, in all the duties thereof, publick and private, both to ourselves, and to all other congregations of his people, according to the riches and excellency of the gospel, this day celebrated and enjoyed.

And because we have been unprofitable hearers in times past, and now cannot of ourselves receive, as we should, the deep things of God, the mysteries of Jesus Christ, which require a spiritual discerning; to pray, that the Lord, who teacheth to profit, would graciously please to pour out the Spirit of grace, together with the outward means thereof, causing us to attain such a measure of the excellency of the knowledge of Christ Jesus our Lord, and, in him, of the things which belong to our peace, that we may account all things but as dross in comparison of him; and that we, tasting the first-fruits of the glory that is to be revealed, may long for a more full and perfect communion with him, that where he is, we may be also, and enjoy the fulness of those joys and pleasures which are at his right hand for evermore.

More particularly, that God would in a special manner furnish his servant (now called to dispense the bread of life unto his household) with wisdom, fidelity, zeal, and utterance, that he may divide the word of God aright, to every one his portion, in evidence and demonstration of the Spirit and power; and that the Lord would circumcise the ears and hearts of the hearers, to hear, love, and receive with meekness the ingrafted word, which is able to save their souls; make them as good ground to receive in the good seed of the word, and strengthen them against the temptations of Satan, the cares of the world, the hardness of their own hearts, and whatsoever else may hinder their profitable and saving hearing; that so Christ may be so formed in them, and live in them, that all their thoughts may be brought into captivity to the obedience of Christ, and their hearts established in every good word and work for ever."

We judge this to be a convenient order, in the ordinary public prayer; yet so, as the minister may defer (as in prudence he shall think meet) some part of these petitions till after his sermon, or offer up to God some of the thanksgivings hereafter appointed, in his prayer before his sermon.

OF THE PREACHING OF THE WORD

Preaching of the word, being the power of God unto salvation, and one of the greatest and most excellent works belonging to the ministry of the gospel, should be so performed, that the workman need not be ashamed, but may save himself, and those that hear him.

It is presupposed, (according to the rules for ordination,) that the minister of Christ is in some good measure gifted for so weighty a service, by his skill in the original languages, and in such arts and sciences as are handmaids unto divinity; by his knowledge in the whole body of theology, but most of all in the holy scriptures, having his senses and heart exercised in them above the common sort of believers; and by the illumination of God's Spirit, and other gifts of edification, which (together with reading and studying of the word) he ought still to seek by prayer, and an humble heart, resolving to admit and receive any truth not yet attained, whenever God shall make it known unto him. All which he is to make use of, and improve, in his private preparations, before he deliver in public what he hath provided.

Ordinarily, the subject of his sermon is to be some text of scripture, holding forth some principle or head of religion, or suitable to some special occasion emergent; or he may go on in some chapter, psalm, or book of the holy scripture, as he shall see fit.

Let the introduction to his text be brief and perspicuous, drawn from the text itself, or context, or some parallel place, or general sentence of scripture.

If the text be long, (as in histories or parables it sometimes must be,) let him give a brief sum of it; if short, a paraphrase thereof, if need be: in both, looking diligently to the scope of the text, and pointing at the chief heads and grounds of doctrine which he is to raise from it.

In analysing and dividing his text, he is to regard more the order of matter than of words; and neither to burden the memory of the hearers in the beginning with too many members of division, nor to trouble their minds with obscure terms of art.

In raising doctrines from the text, his care ought to be, *First,* That the matter be the truth of God. *Secondly,* That it be a truth contained in or grounded on that text, that the hearers may discern how God teacheth it from thence. *Thirdly,* That he chiefly insist upon those doctrines which are principally intended; and make most for the edification of the hearers.

The doctrine is to be expressed in plain terms; or, if any thing in it need explication, it is to be opened, and the consequence also from the text cleared. The parallel places of scripture, confirming the doctrine, are rather to be plain and pertinent, than many, and (it need be) some what insisted upon, and applied to the purpose in hand.

The arguments or reasons are to be solid, and, as much as may be, convincing. The illustrations, of what kind soever, ought to be full of light, and such as may convey the truth into the hearer's heart with spiritual delight.

If any doubt obvious from scripture, reason, or prejudice of the hearers, seem to arise, it is very requisite to remove it, by reconciling the seeming differences, answering the reasons, and discovering and taking away the causes of prejudice and mistake. Otherwise it is not fit to detain the hearers with propounding or answering vain or wicked cavils, which, as they are endless, so the propounding and answering of them doth more hinder than promote edification.

He is not to rest in general doctrine, although never so much cleared and confirmed, but to bring it home to special use, by application to his hearers: which albeit it prove a work of great difficulty to himself, requiring much prudence, zeal, and meditation, and to the natural and corrupt man will be very unpleasant; yet he is to endeavour to perform it in such a manner, that his auditors may feel the word of God to be quick and powerful, and a discerner of the thoughts and intents of the heart; and that, if any unbeliever or ignorant person be present, he may have the secrets of his heart made manifest, and give glory to God.

In the use of instruction or information in the knowledge of some truth, which is a consequence from his doctrine, he may (when convenient) confirm it by a few firm arguments from the text in hand, and other places of scripture, or from the nature of that common-place in divinity, whereof that truth is a branch.

In confutation of false doctrines, he is neither to raise an old heresy from the grave, nor to mention a blasphemous opinion unnecessarily: but, if the people be in danger of an error, he is to confute it soundly, and endeavour to satisfy their judgments and consciences against all objections.

In exhorting to duties, he is, as he seeth cause, to teach also the means that help to the performance of them.

In dehortation, reprehension, and publick admonition, (which require special wisdom,) let him, as there shall be cause, not only discover the nature and greatness of the sin, with the misery attending it, but also shew the danger his hearers are in to be overtaken and surprised by it, together with the remedies and best way to avoid it.

In applying comfort, whether general against all temptations, or particular against some special troubles or terrors, he is carefully to answer such objections as a troubled heart and afflicted spirit may suggest to the contrary. It is also sometimes requisite to give some notes of trial, (which is very profitable, especially when performed by able and experienced ministers, with circumspection and prudence, and the signs clearly grounded on the holy scripture,) whereby the hearers may be able to examine themselves whether they have attained those graces, and performed those duties, to which he exhorteth, or be guilty of the sin reprehended, and in danger of the judgments threatened, or are such to whom the consolations propounded do belong; that accordingly they may be quickened and excited to duty, humbled for their wants and sins, affected with their danger, and strengthened with comfort, as their condition, upon examination, shall require.

And, as he needeth not always to prosecute every doctrine which lies in his text, so is he wisely to make choice of such uses, as, by his residence and conversing with his flock, he findeth most needful and seasonable; and, amongst these, such as may most draw their souls to Christ, the fountain of light, holiness, and comfort.

This method is not prescribed as necessary for every man, or upon every text; but only recommended, as being found by experience to be very much blessed of God, and very helpful for the people's understandings and memories.

But the servant of Christ, whatever his method be, is to perform his whole ministry:

1. Painfully, not doing the work of the Lord negligently.

2. Plainly, that the meanest may understand; delivering the truth not in the enticing words of man's wisdom, but in demonstration of the Spirit and of power, lest the cross of Christ should be made of none effect; abstaining also from an unprofitable use of unknown tongues, strange phrases, and cadences of sounds and words; sparingly citing sentences of ecclesiastical or other human writers, ancient or modern, be they never so elegant.

3. Faithfully, looking at the honour of Christ, the conversion, edification, and salvation of the people, not at his own gain or glory; keeping nothing back which may promote those holy ends, giving to every one his own portion, and bearing indifferent respect unto all, without neglecting the meanest, or sparing the greatest, in their sins.

4. Wisely, framing all his doctrines, exhortations, and especially his reproofs, in such a manner as may be most likely to prevail; shewing all due respect to each man's person and place, and not mixing his own passion or bitterness.

5. Gravely, as becometh the word of God; shunning all such gesture, voice, and expressions, as may occasion the corruptions of men to despise him and his ministry.

6. With loving affection, that the people may see all coming from his godly zeal, and hearty desire to do them good. And,

7. As taught of God, and persuaded in his own heart, that all that he teacheth is the truth of Christ; and walking before his flock, as an example to them in it; earnestly, both in private and publick, recommending his labours to the blessing of God, and watchfully looking to himself, and the flock whereof the Lord hath made him overseer: So shall the doctrine of truth be preserved uncorrupt, many souls converted and built up, and himself receive manifold

comforts of his labours even in this life, and afterward the crown of glory laid up for him in the world to come.

Where there are more ministers in a congregation than one, and they of different gifts, each may more especially apply himself to doctrine or exhortation, according to the gift wherein he most excelleth, and as they shall agree between themselves.

OF PRAYER AFTER SERMON

THE sermon being ended, the minister is "To give thanks for the great love of God, in sending his Son Jesus Christ unto us; for the communication of his Holy Spirit; for the light and liberty of the glorious gospel, and the rich and heavenly blessings revealed therein; as, namely, election, vocation, adoption, justification, sanctification, and hope of glory; for the admirable goodness of God in freeing the land from antichristian darkness and tyranny, and for all other national deliverances; for the reformation of religion; for the covenant; and for many temporal blessings.

To pray for the continuance of the gospel, and all ordinances thereof, in their purity, power, and liberty: to turn the chief and most useful heads of the sermon into some few petitions; and to pray that it may abide in the heart, and bring forth fruit.

To pray for preparation for death and judgment, and a watching for the coming of our Lord Jesus Christ: to entreat of God the forgiveness of the iniquities of our holy things, and the acceptation of our spiritual sacrifice, through the merit and mediation of our great High Priest and Saviour the Lord Jesus Christ."

And because the prayer which Christ taught his disciples is not only a pattern of prayer, but itself a most comprehensive prayer, we recommend it also to be used in the prayers of the church. And whereas, at the administration of the sacraments, the holding publick fasts and days of thanksgiving, and other special occasions, which may afford matter of special petitions and thanksgivings, it is requisite to express somewhat in our publick prayers, (as at this time it is our duty to pray for a blessing upon the Assembly of Divines, the armies by sea and land, for the defence of the King, Parliament, and Kingdom,) every minister is herein to apply himself in his prayer, before or after sermon, to those occasions: but, for the manner, he is left to his liberty, as God shall direct and enable him in piety and wisdom to discharge his duty.

The prayer ended, let a psalm be sung, if with conveniency it may be done. After which (unless some other ordinance of Christ, that concerneth the congregation at that time, be to follow) let the minister dismiss the congregation with a solemn blessing.

Of The Administration
Of The Sacraments:

AND FIRST, OF BAPTISM

Baptism, as it is not unnecessarily to be delayed, so it is not to be administered in any case by any private person, but by a minister of Christ, called to be the steward of the mysteries of God.

Nor is it to be administered in private places, or privately, but in the place of publick worship, and in the face of the congregation, where the people may most conveniently see and hear; and not in the places where fonts, in the time of Popery, were unfitly and superstitiously placed.

The child to be baptized after notice given to the minister the day before, is to be presented by the father, or (in case of his necessary absence) by some Christian friend in his place, professing his earnest desire that the child may be baptized.

Before baptism, the minister is to use some words of instruction, touching the institution, nature, use, and ends of this sacrament, shewing,

"That it is instituted by our Lord Jesus Christ: That it is a seal of the covenant of grace, of our ingrafting into Christ, and of our union with him, of remission of sins, regeneration, adoption, and life eternal: That the water, in baptism, representeth and signifieth both the blood of Christ, which taketh away all guilt of sin, original and actual; and the sanctifying virtue of the Spirit of Christ against the dominion of sin, and the corruption of our sinful nature: That baptizing, or sprinkling and washing with water, signifieth the cleansing from sin by the blood and for the merit of Christ, together with the mortification of sin, and rising from sin to newness of life, by virtue of the death and resurrection of Christ: That the promise is made to believers and their seed; and that the seed and posterity of the faithful, born within the church, have, by their birth, interest in the covenant, and right to the seal of it, and to the outward privileges of the church, under the gospel, no less than the children of Abraham in the time of the Old Testament; the covenant of grace, for substance, being the same; and the grace of God, and the consolation of believers, more plentiful than before: That the Son of God admitted little children into his presence, embracing and blessing them, saying, *For of such is the kingdom of God:* That children, by baptism, are solemnly received into the bosom of the visible church, distinguished from the world, and them that are without, and united with believers; and that all who are baptized in the name of Christ, do renounce, and by their baptism are bound to fight against the devil, the world, and the flesh: That they are Christians, and federally holy before baptism, and therefore are they baptized: That the inward grace and virtue of baptism is not tied to that very moment of time wherein it is administered; and that the fruit and power thereof reacheth to the whole course of our life; and that outward baptism is not so necessary, that, through the want thereof, the infant is in danger of damnation, or the parents guilty, if they do not contemn or neglect the ordinance of Christ, when and where it may be had."

In these or the like instructions, the minister is to use his own liberty and godly wisdom, as the ignorance or errors in the doctrine of baptism, and the edification of the people, shall require.

He is also to admonish all that are present,

"To look back to their baptism; to repent of their sins against their covenant with God; to stir up their faith; to improve and make right use of their baptism, and of the covenant sealed thereby betwixt God and their souls."

He is to exhort the parent,

> "To consider the great mercy of God to him and his child; to bring up the child in the knowledge of the grounds of the Christian religion, "and in the nurture and admonition of the Lord; and to let him know the danger of God's wrath to himself and child, if he be negligent: requiring his solemn promise for the performance of his duty."

This being done, prayer is also to be joined with the word of institution, for sanctifying the water to this spiritual use; and the minister is to pray to this or the like effect:

> "That the Lord, who hath not left us as strangers without the covenant of promise, but called us to the privileges of his ordinances, would graciously vouchsafe to sanctify and bless his own ordinance of baptism at this time: That he would join the inward baptism of his Spirit with the outward baptism of water; make this baptism to the infant a seal of adoption, remission of sin, regeneration, and eternal life, and all other promises of the covenant of grace: That the child may be planted into the likeness of the death and resurrection of Christ; and that, the body of sin being destroyed in him, he may serve God in newness of life all his days."

Then the minister is to demand the name of the child; which being told him, he is to say, (calling the child by his name,)

> *I baptize thee in the name of the Father, and of the Son, and of the Holy Ghost.*

As he pronounceth these words, he is to baptize the child with water: which, for the manner of doing of it, is not only lawful but sufficient, and most expedient to be, by pouring or sprinkling of the water on the face of the child, without adding any other ceremony.

This done, he is to give thanks and pray, to this or the like purpose:

"Acknowledging with all thankfulness, that the Lord is true and faithful in keeping covenant and mercy: That he is good and gracious, not only in that he numbereth us among his saints, but is pleased also to bestow upon our children this singular token and badge of his love in Christ: That, in his truth and special providence, he daily bringeth some into the bosom of his church, to be partakers of his inestimable benefits, purchased by the blood of his dear Son, for the continuance and increase of his church.

And praying, That the Lord would still continue, and daily confirm more and more this his unspeakable favour: That he would receive the infant now baptized, and solemnly entered into the household of faith, into his fatherly tuition and defence, and remember him with the favour that he sheweth to his people; that, if he shall be taken out of this life in his infancy, the Lord, who is rich in mercy, would be pleased to receive him up into glory; and if he live, and attain the years of discretion, that the Lord would so teach him by his word and Spirit, and make his baptism effectual to him, and so uphold him by his divine power and grace, that by faith he may prevail against the devil, the world, and the flesh, till in the end he obtain a full and final victory, and so be kept by the power of God through faith unto salvation, through Jesus Christ our Lord."

OF THE CELEBRATION OF THE COMMUNION, OR SACRAMENT OF THE LORD'S SUPPER.

THE communion, or supper of the Lord, is frequently to be celebrated; but how often, may be considered and determined by the ministers, and other church-governors of each congregation, as they shall find most convenient for the comfort and edification of the people committed to their charge. And, when it shall be administered, we judge it convenient to be done after the morning sermon.

The ignorant and the scandalous are not fit to receive the sacrament of the Lord's Supper.

Where this sacrament cannot with convenience be frequently administered, it is requisite that publick warning be given the sabbath-day before the administration thereof: and that either then, or on some day of that week, something concerning that ordinance, and the due preparation thereunto, and participation thereof, be taught; that, by the diligent use of all means sanctified of God to that end, both in publick and private, all may come better prepared to that heavenly feast.

When the day is come for administration, the minister, having ended his sermon and prayer, shall make a short exhortation:

"Expressing the inestimable benefit we have by this sacrament, together with the ends and use thereof: setting forth the great necessity of having our comforts and strength renewed thereby in this our pilgrimage and warfare: how necessary it is that we come unto it with knowledge, faith, repentance, love, and with hungering and thirsting souls after Christ and his benefits: how great the danger to eat and drink unworthily.

Next, he is, in the name of Christ, on the one part, to warn all such as are ignorant, scandalous, profane, or that live in any sin or offence against their knowledge or conscience, that they presume not to come to that holy table; shewing them, that he that eateth and drinketh unworthily, eateth and drinketh judgment unto himself: and, on the other part, he is in an especial manner to invite and encourage all that labour under the sense of the burden of their sins, and fear of wrath, and desire to reach out unto a greater progress in grace than yet they can attain unto, to come to the Lord's table; assuring them, in the same name, of ease, refreshing, and strength to their weak and wearied souls."

After this exhortation, warning, and invitation, the table being before decently covered, and so conveniently placed, that the communicants may orderly sit about it, or at it, the minister is to begin the action with sanctifying and blessing the elements of bread and wine set before him, (the bread in comely and convenient vessels, so prepared, that, being broken by him, and given, it may be distributed amongst the communicants; the wine also in large cups,) having first, in a few words, shewed that those elements, otherwise common, are now set apart and sanctified to this holy use, by the word of institution and prayer.

Let the words of institution be read out of the Evangelists, or out of the first Epistle of the Apostle Paul to the Corinthians, Chapter 11:23. *I have received of the Lord, &c.* to the 27th Verse, which the minister may, when he seeth requisite, explain and apply.

Let the prayer, thanksgiving, or blessing of the bread and wine, be to this effect:

"With humble and hearty acknowledgment of the greatness of our misery, from which neither I/man; nor angel was able to deliver us, and of our great unworthiness of the least of all God's mercies; to give thanks to God for all his benefits, and especially for that great benefit of our redemption, the love of God the Father, the sufferings and merits of the Lord Jesus Christ the Son of God, by which we are delivered; and for all means of grace, the word and sacraments; and for this sacrament in particular, by which Christ, and all his benefits, are applied and sealed up unto us, which, notwithstanding the denial of them unto others, are in great mercy continued unto us, after so much and long abuse of them all.

To profess that there is no other name under heaven by which we can be saved, but the name of Jesus Christ, by whom alone we receive liberty and life, have access to the throne of grace, are admitted to eat and drink at his own table, and are sealed up by his Spirit to an assurance of happiness and everlasting life.

Earnestly to pray to God, the Father of all mercies, and God of all consolation, to vouchsafe his gracious presence, and the effectual working of his Spirit in us; and so to sanctify these elements both of bread and wine, and to bless his own ordinance, that we may receive by faith the body and blood of Jesus Christ, crucified for us, and so to feed upon him, that he may be one with us, and we one with him; that he may live in us, and we in him, and to him who hath loved us, and given himself for us."

All which he is to endeavour to perform with suitable affections, answerable to such an holy action, and to stir up the like in the people.

The elements being now sanctified by the word and prayer, the minister, being at the table, is to take the bread in his hand, and say, in these expressions, (or other the like, used by Christ or his apostle upon this occasion:)

"According to the holy institution, command, and example of our blessed Saviour Jesus Christ, I take this bread, and, having given thanks, break it, and give it unto you; (there the minister, who is also himself to communicate, is to break the bread, and give it to the communicants;) *"Take ye, eat ye; this is the body of Christ which is broken for you: do this in remembrance of him."*

In like manner the minister is to take the cup, and say, in these expressions, (or other the like, used by Christ or the apostle upon the same occasion:)

"According to the institution, command, and example of our Lord Jesus Christ, I take this cup, and give it unto you; (here he giveth it to the communicants;) *This cup is the new testament in the blood of Christ, which is shed for the remission of the sins of many: drink ye all of it."*

After all have communicated, the minister may, in a few words, put them in mind,

"Of the grace of God in Jesus Christ, held forth in this sacrament; and exhort them to walk worthy of it."

The minister is to give solemn thanks to God,

"For his rich mercy, and invaluable goodness, vouchsafed to them in that sacrament; and to entreat for pardon for the defects of the whole service, and for the gracious assistance of his good Spirit, whereby they may be enabled to walk in the strength of that grace, as becometh those who have received so great pledges of salvation."

The collection for the poor is so to be ordered, that no part of the publick worship be thereby hindered.

OF THE SANCTIFICATION
OF THE
LORD'S DAY

THE Lord's day ought to be so remembered before-hand, as that all worldly business of our ordinary callings may be so ordered, and so timely and seasonably laid aside, as they may not be impediments to the due sanctifying of the day when it comes.

The whole day is to be celebrated as holy to the Lord, both in publick and private, as being the Christian sabbath. To which end, it is requisite, that there be a holy cessation or resting all that day from all unnecessary labours; and an abstaining, not only from all sports and pastimes, but also from all worldly words and thoughts.

That the diet on that day be so ordered, as that neither servants be unnecessarily detained from the publick worship of God, nor any other person hindered from the sanctifying that day. That there be private preparations of every person and family, by prayer for themselves, and for God's assistance of the minister, and for a blessing upon his ministry; and by such other holy exercises, as may further dispose them to a more comfortable communion with God in his public ordinances.

That all the people meet so timely for publick worship, that the whole congregation may be present at the beginning, and with one heart solemnly join together in all parts of the publick worship, and not depart till after the blessing.

That what time is vacant, between or after the solemn meetings of the congregation in publick, be spent in reading, meditation, repetition of sermons; especially by calling their families to an account of what they have heard, and catechising of them, holy conferences, prayer for a blessing upon the publick ordinances, singing of psalms, visiting the sick, relieving the poor, and such like duties of piety, charity, and mercy, accounting the sabbath a delight.

THE SOLEMNIZATION OF MARRIAGE

ALTHOUGH marriage be no sacrament, nor peculiar to the church of God, but common to mankind, and of publick interest in every commonwealth; yet, because such as marry are to marry in the Lord, and have special need of instruction, direction, and exhortation, from the word of God, at their entering into such a new condition, and of the blessing of God upon them therein, we judge it expedient that marriage be solemnized by a lawful minister of the word, that he may accordingly counsel them, and pray for a blessing upon them.

Marriage is to be betwixt one man and one woman only; and they such as are not within the degrees of consanguinity or affinity prohibited by the word of God; and the parties are to be of years of discretion, fit to make their own choice, or, upon good grounds, to give their mutual consent.

Before the solemnizing of marriage between any persons, the purpose of marriage shall be published by the minister three several sabbath-days, in the congregation, at the place or places of their most usual and constant abode, respectively. And of this publication the minister who is to join them in marriage shall have sufficient testimony, before he proceed to solemnize the marriage.

Before that publication of such their purpose, (if the parties be under age,) the consent of the parents, or others under whose power they are, (in case the parents be dead,) is to be made known to the church officers of that congregation, to be recorded.

The like is to be observed in the proceedings of all others, although of age, whose parents are living, for their first marriage.

And, in after marriages of either of those parties, they shall be exhorted not to contract marriage without first acquainting their parents with it, (if with conveniency it may be done,) endeavouring to obtain their consent.

Parents ought not to force their children to marry without their free consent, nor deny their own consent without just cause.

After the purpose or contract of marriage hath been thus published, the marriage is not to be long deferred. Therefore the minister, having had convenient warning, and nothing being objected to hinder it, is publickly to solemnize it in the place appointed by authority for publick worship, before a competent number of credible witnesses, at some convenient hour of the day, at any time of the year, except on a day of publick humiliation. And we advise that it be not on the Lord's day.

And because all relations are sanctified by the word and prayer, the minister is to pray for a blessing upon them, to this effect:

"Acknowledging our sins, whereby we have made ourselves less than the least of all the mercies of God, and provoked him to embitter all our comforts; earnestly, in the name of Christ, to entreat the Lord (whose presence and favour is the happiness of every condition, and sweetens every relation) to be their portion, and to own and accept them in Christ, who are now to be joined in the honourable estate of marriage, the covenant of their God: and that, as he hath brought them together by his providence, he would sanctify them by his Spirit, giving them a new frame of heart fit for their new estate; enriching them with all graces whereby they may perform the duties, enjoy the comforts, undergo the cares, and resist the temptations which accompany that condition, as becometh Christians."

The prayer being ended, it is convenient that the minister do briefly declare unto them, out of the scripture,

"The institution, use, and ends of marriage, with the conjugal duties, which, in all faithfulness, they are to perform each to other; exhorting them to study the holy word of God, that they may learn to live by faith, and to be content in the midst of all marriage cares and troubles, sanctifying God's name, in a thankful, sober, and holy use of all conjugal comforts; praying much with and for one another; watching over and provoking each other to love and good works; and to live together as the heirs of the grace of life."

After solemn charging of the persons to be married, before the great God, who searcheth all hearts, and to whom they must give a strict account at the last day, that if either of them know any cause, by precontract or otherwise, why they may not lawfully proceed to marriage, that they now discover it; the minister (if no impediment be acknowledged) shall cause first the man to take the woman by the right hand, saying these words:

I N. do take thee N. to be my married wife, and do, in the presence of God, and before this congregation, promise and covenant to be a loving and faithful husband unto thee, until God shall separate us by death.

Then the woman shall take the man by the right hand, and say these words:

I N. do take thee N. to be my married husband, and I do, in the presence of God, and before this congregation, promise and covenant to be a loving, faithful, and obedient wife unto thee, until God shall separate us by death.

Then, without any further ceremony, the minister shall, in the face of the congregation, pronounce them to be husband and wife, according to God's ordinance; and so conclude the action with prayer to this effect:

> "That the Lord would be pleased to accompany his own ordinance with his blessing, beseeching him to enrich the persons now married, as with other pledges of his love, so particularly with the comforts and fruits of marriage, to the praise of his abundant mercy, in and through Christ Jesus."

A register is to be carefully kept, wherein the names of the parties so married, with the time of their marriage, are forthwith to be fairly recorded in a book provided for that purpose, for the perusal of all whom it may concern.

CONCERNING VISITATION OF THE SICK

It is the duty of the minister not only to teach the people committed to his charge in publick, but privately; and particularly to admonish, exhort, reprove, and comfort them, upon all seasonable occasions, so far as his time, strength, and personal safety will permit.

He is to admonish them, in time of health, to prepare for death; and, for that purpose, they are often to confer with their minister about the estate of their souls; and, in times of sickness, to desire his advice and help, timely and seasonably, before their strength and understanding fail them.

Times of sickness and affliction are special opportunities put into his hand by God to minister a word in season to weary souls: because then the consciences of men are or should be more awakened to bethink themselves of their spiritual estate for eternity; and Satan also takes advantage then to load them more with sore and heavy temptations: therefore the minister, being sent for, and repairing to the sick, is to apply himself, with all tenderness and love, to administer some spiritual good to his soul, to this effect.

He may, from the consideration of the present sickness, instruct him out of scripture, that diseases come not by chance, or by distempers of body only, but by the wise and orderly guidance of the good hand of God to every particular person smitten by them. And that, whether it be laid upon him out of displeasure for sin, for his correction and amendment, or for trial and exercise of his graces, or for other special and excellent ends, all his sufferings shall turn to his profit, and work together for his good, if he sincerely labour to make a sanctified use of God's visitation, neither despising his chastening, nor waxing weary of his correction.

If he suspect him of ignorance, he shall examine him in the principles of religion, especially touching repentance and faith; and, as he seeth cause, instruct him in the nature, use, excellency, and necessity of those graces; as also touching the covenant of grace; and Christ the Son of God, the Mediator of it; and concerning remission of sins by faith in him.

He shall exhort the sick person to examine himself, to search and try his former ways, and his estate towards God.

And if the sick person shall declare any scruple, doubt, or temptation that are upon him, instructions and resolutions shall be given to satisfy and settle him.

If it appear that he hath not a due sense of his sins, endeavours ought to be used to convince him of his sins, of the guilt and desert of them; of the filth and pollution which the soul contracts by them; and of the curse of the law, and wrath of God, due to them; that he may be truly affected with and humbled for them: and withal make known the danger of deferring repentance, and of neglecting salvation at any time offered; to awaken his conscience, and rouse him up out of a stupid and secure condition, to apprehend the justice and wrath of God, before whom none can stand, but he that, lost in himself, layeth hold upon Christ by faith.

If he hath endeavoured to walk in the ways of holiness, and to serve God in uprightness, although not without many failings and infirmities; or, if his spirit be broken with the sense of sin, or cast down through want of the sense of God's favour; then it will be fit to raise him up, by setting before him the freeness and fulness of God's grace, the sufficiency of righteousness in Christ, the gracious offers in the gospel, that all who repent, and believe with all their heart in God's mercy through Christ, renouncing their own righteousness, shall have life and salvation in him. It may be also useful to shew him, that death hath in it no spiritual evil to be feared by those that are in Christ, because sin, the sting of death, is taken away by Christ, who hath delivered all that are his from the bondage of the fear of death, triumphed over the grave, given us victory, is himself entered into glory to prepare a place for his people: so that neither life nor death shall be able to separate them from God's love in Christ, in whom such are sure, though now they must be laid in the dust, to obtain a joyful and glorious resurrection to eternal life.

Advice also may be given, as to beware of an ill-grounded persuasion on mercy, or on the goodness of his condition for heaven, so to disclaim all merit in himself, and to cast himself wholly upon God for mercy, in the sole merits and mediation of Jesus Christ, who hath engaged himself never to cast off them who in truth and sincerity come unto him. Care also must be taken, that the sick person be not cast down into despair, by such a severe representation of the wrath of God due to him for his sins, as is not mollified by a sensible propounding of Christ and his merit for a door of hope to every penitent believer.

When the sick person is best composed, may be least disturbed, and other necessary offices about him least hindered, the minister, if desired, shall pray with him, and for him, to this effect:

117

"Confessing and bewailing of sin original and actual; the miserable condition of all by nature, as being children of wrath, and under the curse; acknowledging that all diseases, sicknesses, death, and hell itself, are the proper issues and effects thereof; imploring God's mercy for the sick person, through the blood of Christ; beseeching that God would open his eyes, discover unto him his sins, cause him to see himself lost in himself, make known to him the cause why God smiteth him, reveal Jesus Christ to his soul for righteousness and life, give unto him his Holy Spirit, to create and strengthen faith to lay hold upon Christ, to work in him comfortable evidences of his love, to arm him against temptations, to take off his heart from the world, to sanctify his present visitation, to furnish him with patience and strength to bear it, and to give him perseverance in faith to the end.

That, if God shall please to add to his days, he would vouchsafe to bless and sanctify all means of his recovery; to remove the disease, renew his strength, and enable him to walk worthy of God, by a faithful remembrance, and diligent observing of such vows and promises of holiness and obedience, as men are apt to make in times of sickness, that he may glorify God in the remaining part of his life.

And, if God have determined to finish his days by the present visitation, he may find such evidence of the pardon of all his sins, of his interest in Christ, and eternal life by Christ, as may cause his inward man to be renewed, while his outward man decayeth; that he may behold death without fear, cast himself wholly upon Christ without doubting, desire to be dissolved and to be with Christ, and so receive the end of his faith, the salvation of his soul, through the only merits and intercession of the Lord Jesus Christ, our alone Saviour and all-sufficient Redeemer."

The minister shall admonish him also (as there shall be cause) to set his house in order, thereby to prevent inconveniences; to take care for payment of his debts, and to make restitution or satisfaction where he hath done any wrong; to be reconciled to those with whom he hath been at variance, and fully to forgive all men their trespasses against him, as he expects forgiveness at the hand of God.

Lastly, The minister may improve the present occasion to exhort those about the sick person to consider their own mortality, to return to the Lord, and make peace with him; in health to prepare for sickness, death, and judgment; and all the days of their appointed time so to wait until their change come, that when Christ, who is our life, shall appear, they may appear with him in glory.

CONCERNING BURIAL OF THE DEAD

WHEN any person departeth this life, let the dead body, upon the day of burial, be decently attended from the house to the place appointed for publick burial, and there immediately interred, without any ceremony.

And because the custom of kneeling down, and praying by or towards the dead corpse, and other such usages, in the place where it lies before it be carried to burial, are superstitious; and for that praying, reading, and singing, both in going to and at the grave, have been grossly abused, are no way beneficial to the dead, and have proved many ways hurtful to the living; therefore let all such things be laid aside.

Howbeit, we judge it very convenient, that the Christian friends, which accompany the dead body to the place appointed for publick burial, do apply themselves to meditations and conferences suitable to the occasion and that the minister, as upon other occasions, so at this time, if he be present, may put them in remembrance of their duty.

That this shall not extend to deny any civil respects or deferences at the burial, suitable to the rank and condition of the party deceased, while he was living.

CONCERNING PUBLICK SOLEMN FASTING

WHEN some great and notable judgments are either inflicted upon a people, or apparently imminent, or by some extraordinary provocations notoriously deserved; as also when some special blessing is to be sought and obtained, publick solemn fasting (which is to continue the whole day) is a duty that God expecteth from that nation or people.

A religious fast requires total abstinence, not only from all food, (unless bodily weakness do manifestly disable from holding out till the fast be ended, in which case somewhat may be taken, yet very sparingly, to support nature, when ready to faint,) but also from all worldly labour, discourses, and thoughts, and from all bodily delights, and such like, (although at other times lawful,) rich apparel, ornaments, and such like, during the fast; and much more from whatever is in the nature or use scandalous and offensive, as gaudish attire, lascivious habits and gestures, and other vanities of either sex; which we recommend to all ministers, in their places, diligently and zealously to reprove, as at other times, so especially at a fast, without respect of persons, as there shall be occasion.

Before the publick meeting, each family and person apart are privately to use all religious care to prepare their hearts to such a solemn work, and to be early at the congregation.

So large a portion of the day as conveniently may be, is to be spent in publick reading and preaching of the word, with singing of psalms, fit to quicken affections suitable to such a duty: but especially in prayer, to this or the like effect:

121

"Giving glory to the great Majesty of God, the Creator, Preserver, and supreme Ruler of all the world, the better to affect us thereby with an holy reverence and awe of him; acknowledging his manifold, great, and tender mercies, especially to the church and nation, the more effectually to soften and abase our hearts before him; humbly confessing of sins of all sorts, with their several aggravations; justifying God's righteous judgments, as being far less than our sins do deserve; yet humbly and earnestly imploring his mercy and grace for ourselves, the church and nation, for our king, and all in authority, and for all others for whom we are bound to pray, (according as the present exigent requireth,) with more special importunity and enlargement than at other times; applying by faith the promises and goodness of God for pardon, help, and deliverance from the evils felt, feared, or deserved; and for obtaining the blessings which we need and expect; together with a giving up of ourselves wholly and for ever unto the Lord."

In all these, the ministers, who are the mouths of the people unto God, ought so to speak from their hearts, upon serious and thorough premeditation of them, that both themselves and their people may be much affected, and even melted thereby, especially with sorrow for their sins; that it may be indeed a day of deep humiliation and afflicting of the soul.

Special choice is to be made of such scriptures to be read, and of such tests for preaching, as may best work the hearts of the hearers to the special business of the day, and most dispose them to humiliation and repentance: insisting most on those particulars which each minister's observation and experience tells him are most conducing to the edification and reformation of that congregation to which he preacheth.

Before the close of the publick duties, the minister is, in his own and the people's name, to engage his and their hearts to be the Lord's, with professed purpose and resolution to reform whatever is amiss among them, and more particularly such sins as they have been more remarkably guilty of; and to draw near unto God, and to walk more closely and faithfully with him in new obedience, than ever before.

He is also to admonish the people, with all importunity, that the work of that day doth not end with the publick duties of it, but that they are so to improve the remainder of the day, and of their whole life, in reinforcing upon themselves and their families in private all those godly affections and resolutions which they professed in publick, as that they may be settled in their hearts for ever, and themselves may more sensibly find that God hath smelt a sweet savour in Christ from their performances, and is pacified towards them, by answers of grace, in pardoning of sin, in removing of judgments, in averting or preventing of plagues, and in conferring of blessings, suitable to the conditions and prayers of his people, by Jesus Christ.

Besides solemn and general fasts enjoined by authority, we judge that, at other times, congregations may keep days of fasting, as divine providence shall administer unto them special occasion; and also that families may do the same, so it be not on days wherein the congregation to which they do belong is to meet for fasting, or other publick duties of worship.

CONCERNING THE OBSERVATION OF DAYS
OF
PUBLICK THANKSGIVING

WHEN any such day is to be kept, let notice be given of it, and of the occasion thereof, some convenient time before, that the people may the better prepare themselves thereunto.

The day being come, and the congregation (after private preparations) being assembled, the minister is to begin with a word of exhortation, to stir up the people to the duty for which they are met, and with a short prayer for God's assistance and blessing, (as at other conventions for publick worship,) according to the particular occasion of their meeting.

Let him then make some pithy narration of the deliverance obtained, or mercy received, or of whatever hath occasioned that assembling of the congregation, that all may better understand it, or be minded of it, and more affected with it.

And, because singing of psalms is of all other the most proper ordinance for expressing of joy and thanksgiving, let some pertinent psalm or psalms be sung for that purpose, before or after the reading of some portion of the word suitable to the present business.

Then let the minister, who is to preach, proceed to further exhortation and prayer before his sermon, with special reference to the present work: after which, let him preach upon some text of Scripture pertinent to the occasion.

The sermon ended, let him not only pray, as at other times after preaching is directed, with remembrance of the necessities of the Church, King, and State, (if before the sermon they were omitted,) but enlarge himself in due and solemn thanksgiving for former mercies and deliverances; but more especially for that which at the present calls them together to give thanks: with humble petition for the continuance and renewing of God's wonted mercies, as need shall be, and for sanctifying grace to make a right use thereof. And so, having sung another psalm, suitable to the mercy, let him dismiss the congregation with a blessing, that they may have some convenient time for their repast and refreshing.

But the minister (before their dismission) is solemnly to admonish them to beware of all excess and riot, tending to gluttony or drunkenness, and much more of these sins themselves, in their eating and refreshing; and to take care that their mirth and rejoicing be not carnal, but spiritual, which may make God's praise to be glorious, and themselves humble and sober; and that both their feeding and rejoicing may render them more cheerful and enlarged, further to celebrate his praises in the midst of the congregation, when they return unto it in the remaining part of that day.

When the congregation shall be again assembled, the like course in praying, reading, preaching, singing of psalms, and offering up of more praise and thanksgiving, that is before directed for the morning, is to be renewed and continued, so far as the time will give leave.

At one or both of the publick meetings that day, a collection is to be made for the poor, (and in the like manner upon the day of publick humiliation,) that their loins may bless us, and rejoice the more with us. And the people are to be exhorted, at the end of the latter meeting, to spend the residue of that day in holy duties, and testifications of Christian love and charity one towards another, and of rejoicing more and more in the Lord; as becometh those who make the joy of the Lord their strength.

OF SINGING OF PSALMS

IT is the duty of Christians to praise God publickly, by singing of psalms together in the congregation, and also privately in the family.

In singing of psalms, the voice is to be tunably and gravely ordered; but the chief care must be to sing with understanding, and with grace in the heart, making melody unto the Lord.

That the whole congregation may join herein, every one that can read is to have a psalm book; and all others, not disabled by age or otherwise, are to be exhorted to learn to read. But for the present, where many in the congregation cannot read, it is convenient that the minister, or some other fit person appointed by him and the other ruling officers, do read the psalm, line by line, before the singing thereof.

An Appendix:
Touching Days and Places for Publick Worship

THERE is no day commanded in scripture to be kept holy under the gospel but the Lord's day, which is the Christian Sabbath.

Festival days, vulgarly called *Holy-days,* having no warrant in the word of God, are not to be continued.

Nevertheless, it is lawful and necessary, upon special emergent occasions, to separate a day or days for publick fasting or thanksgiving, as the several eminent and extraordinary dispensations of God's providence shall administer cause and opportunity to his people.

As no place is capable of any holiness, under pretence of whatsoever dedication or consecration; so neither is it subject to such pollution by any superstition formerly used, and now laid aside, as may render it unlawful or inconvenient for Christians to meet together therein for the publick worship of God. And therefore we hold it requisite, that the places of publick assembling for worship among us should be continued and employed to that use.

Christian Focus Publications

publishes books for all ages

Our mission statement –

STAYING FAITHFUL

In dependence upon God we seek to help make His infallible Word, the Bible, relevant. Our aim is to ensure that the Lord Jesus Christ is presented as the only hope to obtain forgiveness of sin, live a useful life and look forward to heaven with Him.

REACHING OUT

Christ's last command requires us to reach out to our world with His gospel. We seek to help fulfil that by publishing books that point people towards Jesus and help them develop a Christ-like maturity. We aim to equip all levels of readers for life, work, ministry and mission.

Books in our adult range are published in three imprints.

Christian Focus contains popular works including biographies, commentaries, basic doctrine and Christian living. Our children's books are also published in this imprint.

Mentor focuses on books written at a level suitable for Bible College and seminary students, pastors, and other serious readers. The imprint includes commentaries, doctrinal studies, examination of current issues and church history.

Christian Heritage contains classic writings from the past.

Christian Focus Publications Ltd
Geanies House, Fearn, Ross-shire,
IV20 1TW, Scotland, United Kingdom
info@christianfocus.com
www.christianfocus.com